Lamb at the Altar / the story of a dance

Duke University Press

Durham & London

1994

Lamb at the Altar / the story of a dance

Deborah Hay

Photographs by Phyllis Liedeker

© 1994 Duke University Press

All rights reserved

Printed in the United States of America

on acid-free paper

Typeset in Optima.

Library of Congress Cataloging-in-Publication Data

appear on the last printed page of this book.

All drawings by Deborah Hay. Material from DANCE Music by

Barry Goldensohn (Cummington Press, Omaha, Nebraska, 1992)

reprinted by permission. The movement libretto for *Lamb, Lamb,*

Lamb. . . originally appeared in *The Drama Review,* volume 36,

number 4, reprinted by permission of MIT Press.

For my father,
Joseph Benjamin Goldensohn,
a prince of a dancer
1907–1993

*It is the world of your
own soul you seek.
Only within yourself
exists that other reality
for which you long.
I can give you nothing
that has not already its
own being within
yourself. I can throw
open to you no pic-
ture gallery but your
own soul and all I can
give you is the oppor-
tunity, the impulse,
the key. I help make
your world visible,
that is all.—Herman
Hesse,* Steppenwolf,
*as spoken by the
manager of the Magic
Theater*

Acknowledgments

During the two years that my attention was devoted to writing *Lamb at the Altar / the story of a dance*, numerous people provided practical, personal, technical, and artistic support. Some are people with whom I have had long-lasting friendships, while others simply appeared at the right moment. I am deeply indebted to the places they filled in the process of putting this book together.

I want to acknowledge Phyllis Liedeker for her interest and generosity, which were and continue to be forthcoming in relation to photographing my work, and for permission to use her photographs in *Lamb at the Altar / the story of a dance*.

I wish to thank Johanna Smith for providing the space, comfort, and silence I needed to write; Beverly Bajema, for two years of patient inquiry into my meaning, verifying information, and reading the manuscript aloud to me several times; Barry and Lorrie Goldensohn, my brother and sister-in-law, for teaching me to locate *my* voice; Bill Jeffers, for the many times his computer expertise was hastily called into service; Marsia Hart Reese, for the myriad editing marks she made in the margins and the remarks she embellished them with; Randy Lusk and Judith Sims for being impartial readers; Betty Sue Flowers for her enthusiasm during the earliest stage of this project. I am deeply grateful for the support I have been privileged to receive from the National Endowment for the Arts Dance Program. I do not think the book would have happened without the Endowment's active interest in my dance projects.

The book could not be written without the individuals who made up the *Playing Awake 1991* and *Playing Awake 1992* large-group workshops. In 1991 they were; Rosita Alvarez, Beverly Bajema, Savannah Bradshaw, Janna Buckmaster, Tana Christie, Jean Cornelius, Brenda Cotto-Escalera, Rebecca Fox, Lisa Foster, Liz Gans, Sheri Goodman, Charissa Goodrich, Eric Gould, Heleri, Scott Heron, Tim Hurst, Heather Jarry, Manu Bird Jobst, Namsik Kim, Scott Lehman, Andrew Long, Virginia Maclovia, Chris McCarthy, Jeannie McEwan, Leila McKay, Marta Moncada, Christina Morrison, Lydia Francine Munro, Sheelah Murthy, Mary Owen, Stephanie Britten Phillips, Herb Pike, Charly Raines, Andrew St. Martin, BJ Taylor, Linda Urton, Liliana Valenzuela, Brett Vapnek, Nina Winthrop, Julia Voland, and Ellen Waible.

In 1992 they were Pat Andrus, Myrna Baird, Beverly Bajema, Saraja de Jonge, Hawkeye Glenn, Patricia Greene, Heleri, Grace Mi-He Lee, Christian Leeby, Brian Leonard, Nancy Lewis, Shannon Loch, Christa Masbruch, Jeri Moses, Herb Pike, Charly Raines, and Margery Segal.

Last, I want to thank Harry Porter, who held, humored, fed, and provided diversion for me during this process. And my daughter Savannah, who miraculously escaped learning how to dance, thereby inspiring me to riotously new heights in my appreciation of movement.

Preface

I choreographed *Lamb, lamb . . .* , a dance for forty-one individuals, during a four-month workshop titled *Playing Awake 1991.* The audience who attended the performances of *Lamb, lamb, lamb . . .* , expressed a worshipful fixation in watching a prominently situated male figure, clothed in a white jock strap, who with great passion and sensuality writhed uninterruptedly for an hour. There was another figure, even more prominently situated onstage, present throughout the dance. It was a woman, whose movement direction was to witness and reflect, as simply as possible, whatever she saw in the large cast of dancers onstage. Few people mentioned the subtlety and innuendo evident in her dance. I find this fact to be a yardstick for the time it will take audience and performer to appreciate and explore shade above power from a brilliant sun.

Lamb at the Altar / the story of a dance is about the whole body of a dancer exploring dying. I understand dance to include the action of dying, whether or not I choose to realize it. I am making an effort to come to terms with dying as an experiential process of which I possess negotiable comprehension. I want to include the perception of dying in my performance practice because it invigorates my living each moment. I am not talking about the emotional, psychological, clinical, or cultural attitudes about dying, although I use the energy surrounding these beliefs to fire my attention.

Lamb at the Altar / the story of a dance is about the forty-six people who came to Austin, Texas, from all over the country to take part in *Playing Awake 1991,* a performance workshop for trained and untrained dancers. (I have conducted twelve annual large-group workshops in Austin, Texas, since 1980.) They trusted, and at other times had difficulty trusting, during their four-month commitment to play in the shade of my movement explorations.

Lamb at the Altar / the story of a dance contains a movement libretto with photographs and original drawings, highlighted with the philosophy, stories, and intrigue that influenced the April 1991 premiere of *Lamb, lamb, lamb, lamb, lamb . . . .*

The Afterword reflects changes I made as a dancer, teacher, and choreographer during the *Playing Awake 1992* workshop and concludes with a score for my solo *Lamb at the Altar.*

Lamb at the Altar is the story of a dance. It is my personal tribute to the humor, limitation, and abundance within the particular arrangement of particles that suggest individual identity.

The paragraphs in boldface type signify the movement libretto for the dance *Lamb, lamb, lamb, lamb . . . .* Italicized phrases indicate my performance meditation practices and names given to some of the movements. The regular text represents the stories that bind the performance practices (italics) with the movement libretto (boldface).

Deborah Hay
Austin, Texas

Lamb at the Altar / the story of a dance

There are no funds to commission a composer to create an original work for the large-group workshop performances four months from now. I decide that the dancers will be their own chorus. How to make this happen is beyond me at the moment; I am tone deaf with no background in music theory. Fear and desperation force me to request that we sing "Mary Had a Little Lamb." By the end of our first rehearsal, a childhood tradition is willfully deconstructed.

*Lamb, lamb, lamb...
performed on April
19, 1991, at the
Vortex Performance
Cafe, Austin, Texas.*

Lamb, lamb, lamb, lamb is a rapid, thick-tongued, gentle utterance created inside the mouth cavity. The word *lamb* does not drop or land. Rather, a dancer, with hands poised in front of the lower lip, scoops the word *lamb* back up into the mouth as it falls out.

Lamb appeals to me in this form. The dancers are urged to include the choreographed scooping hand gesture whenever the name of the dance is spoken. I title the dance with an unfixed number of *lambs* so that it is not repeated the same way within a paragraph or a simple conversation.

On February 18, 1991, a month and a half into the four-month workshop, Matthew Fox, a radical Dominican priest, stands before a large Austin audience. Halfway through his talk, he speaks of the mystic interpretation of *lamb* in the Bible as the cosmic child within. Tears spring from my eyes. The timeliness of the information feels like a benediction for *Lamb, lamb, lamb, lamb, lamb, lamb, lamb, lamb, lamb, lamb ....*

a movement libretto for forty-one individuals inspired by the dance *Lamb, lamb, lamb, lamb . . .* premiered in Austin, Texas, April 25-28, 1991

Dying is movement in communion with all there is.

Deborah Hay.
Deborah Hay and
Playing Awake, 1991
workshop partici-
pants at Synergy
Studio, Austin, Texas.

It is January 6th, the first day of the *Playing Awake 1991* workshop. I can't resist the anticipation already in effect, so I get out of bed at 4:30 a.m., shower, dress, sit in the darkness and drink two cups of coffee, hustle out the door, and drive eight miles to the studio. By 6:30 a.m. I use seven calla lilies from last night's dinner party to make the centerpiece for a studio altar. This is the first public altar I prepare in ten years. Candles, shells, a Vermont rock, a tin globe, and a bowl of water surround the flowers on a richly hued Turkish kilim. A photograph of an Indonesian stone figure, smilingly quiet and spine straight in a lotus position, is taped to the green crystal vase holding the lilies. Dark striped silk cloth hangs behind the altar. I purchased the fabric three years earlier when I taught at the School for New Dance Development in Amsterdam.

Beside the vase is a red and blue circus tent music box with a white clown suspended over a stage floor. His knees are jointed, giving movement to his legs as his body bobs to the music. He juggles a yellow ball overhead from one open palm to the other. "DA Da dada DADA / DA Da dada DADA / Da Da DaDA / Da dadadadada" (*Tico Tico*, by Zoquinaba de Abreu). The music box becomes a symbol for the workshop. The clown's short wacky adjustments from side to side, balancing a little bit here and a little bit there, is the same dance that we will practice for the next four months.

It is spring and twilight in Texas. A bleached blue-green sky spreads across an abandoned shopping center parking lot. An ex-

boomtown triplex theater has become the experimental underground Vortex Performance Cafe. The audience begins arriving at 7:30 p.m. The movie house glass doors are pushed open and swing shut for the next forty minutes.

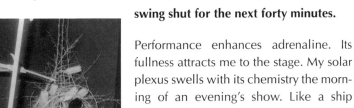

Liz Gans and Lydia Francine Munro in their shacks in the lobby of the Vortex Performance Cafe, April 19, 1991.

Performance enhances adrenaline. Its fullness attracts me to the stage. My solar plexus swells with its chemistry the morning of an evening's show. Like a ship passing along a narrow channel I guide myself through the day. Entering the theater, I notice a further quickening and grab it to clarify my stillness. In the dressing room grooming before the mirror, the adrenalin reddens my cheeks. As I step onto stage, the locks break open and my ship sets sail.

■I move to Austin in 1976, and through 1979 I am frustrated by sporadic attendance in my dance classes. I create options to bypass this behavior. I schedule weekend intensives, three-hour workshops, group dances/not classes, instantaneous performances / not workshops. I clearly remember thinking, "I only want to work with people whose choice to study with me is a priority in their lives for months at a time." Thus the large-group workshop format is born.

In January 1980 it is a revelation to me when thirty-eight people register for my five-month dance workshop scheduled to meet every weekday morning for two hours. In late May of that year, thirty-seven people premier *HEAVEN/below*, an hour-long choreographed dance, performed for the Austin community.■

The role of consciousness is choice.
Consciousness of movement is performance.
A performance meditation practice is the choice of the performer to exercise movement consciousness.

For four months the same performance meditations are collectively practiced by the trained and untrained dancers in *Playing Awake 1991*.

Music, altar, lighting, and incense ease passage into the studio for the forty-three who arrive. Tomorrow we top off with forty-six.

Many students arrive early to stretch or become quiet. Just after 8 a.m. we form a circle and hold hands. This too is a ritual that I abandon ten years ago. During the 1980s I fight the impulse to spiritualize. I do not want to be labeled as cosmic, hippie, or naive. For ten years I subvert evidence of ritual or ceremony. I learn to deliver language simply and directly. But something in me is changed. In 1989 an imaginative dance company board member registers me in Gay Luce's Nine Gates Mystery School, a California-based workshop. It is the first time I participate in a workshop since t'ai chi classes on Canal Street in New York in the mid-sixties. The board member attends Mystery School the previous year and feels that by supporting my presence at this twenty-day intensive, I can potentially incorporate some ineffably potent material into my teaching.

At Mystery School we practice many ancient ceremonies for inducing and participating in universal energy systems. I surrender to suggestion and have ninety percent success. I levitate; see two grandfathers I never met; monitor my soul traveling through the void toward a distant light; envision a close-up magnification of a hawk's feathers, beak, and talons; I see my dead mother entirely alive; I experience prophesy. Now I feel compelled to include this potential for expansion in my teaching. Creating an altar and forming a circle are two such avenues for transmission.

We gather by the altar. I feel a strong urge to express my gratitude and appreciation to the powers, people, and events that bring us together. My embarrassment and apology about publicly enacting a ritual, with no experience except perhaps five minutes on Thanksgiving Day, is agonizing. To add to the discomfort, I am about to ask that everyone present, many whom I am meeting for the first time, follow in kind. My request helps me to recognize that *playing awake* does not discriminate between mystical, earthly, or practical sources of strength.

We discuss living arrangements for the eleven people from out of town, some of whom still need housing. The availability of inexpensive student-like apartments near downtown Austin makes it easy to live within walking distance to the studio where the workshop is located. This is a determining factor in choosing which studio space to rent.

Information about the local job market is pooled for those from out-of-town who need to supplement their income while the workshop is in progress. Many trendsetting restaurants provide part-time employment. There are tutorial, child-care, after-school programs, house-cleaning, and clerical jobs, all offering minimal wages which can nevertheless support Austin's laid-back lifestyle.

A list of logistical workshop tips is given to everyone:
—Get enough sleep the night before so you can be here before eight in order to start with everyone at eight.
—Bring drinking water because the studio air is dry.
—Eat a light breakfast and bring fruit, juice, or a light pick-me-up to help get you through the workshop. There are no breaks.
—Hang coats on the rack in the hallway. Keep other belongings against the south wall of the studio. This way the studio is free of clutter.
—Wear layered clothing.

Tea cakes placed on the altar at eight are eaten by the time the studio empties.

White calla lily flesh appears to resist the advance of time during the first week of *Playing Awake*.

In the lobby, twenty shacks are built with home, street, and studio objects and minimal construction requirements. All materials are, or are painted, white. . . . Virginia Maclovia and Tana Christie reflecting stillness and impermanence.

The only indoor lighting is for a circular concession stand in the middle of the lobby. A seemingly ad hoc arrangement of chairs and tables stands amidst twenty shacks. A volunteer group of *Lamb, lamb . . .* artists build the shacks with home, street, and studio findings and minimal construction requirements. All materials are, or are painted, white. Performers wear white clothes, chosen to expose the neck and limbs.

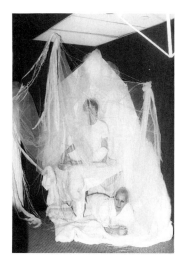

I meet Sheelah Murthy in a performance class I teach at the University of Texas at Austin several years ago. She is an art major who consistently brings unexpected and provocative dances to my class. In addition to performing in *Lamb, lamb . . .* , she designs and coordinates the transformation of the Vortex theater lobby. Only a few shacks reflect what I imagined. I saw a shanty town. Instead the lobby becomes a thematic art installation with a vast amount of personal integrity and imagination built into the quasi-structures.

Sheelah asks Pittsburgh Paint to donate two cans of white paint and several paint brushes to prepare the lobby installation. They request a letter from the director of the nonprofit organization that is seeking the donation. I sit down to my computer and write:

To whom it may concern:

The Deborah Hay Dance Company is requesting the contribution of two gallons of white latex paint, two cans of white spray enamel and three brushes for the Austin, Texas premiere of *Lamb, lamb, lamb, lamb, . . .*

This dance is choreographed by Deborah Hay and performed by a cast of forty individuals of all ages and backgrounds. Since 1976 Ms. Hay has performed in Austin at the Paramount Theater, Auditorium Shores, Ballet Austin Studio, Capital City Playhouse, SouthPark Skating Rink, Studio D, Nierika Studio, the Crystal Ballroom of the Driskill Hotel, the Hyde Park Theater, Mary Moody Northen Theater at St. Edwards's University, the outdoor theater in Zilker Park, the grand ballroom of the Hilton Hotel on Town Lake, South Austin Recreation Center, the State Theater, Dougherty Arts Center, the B. Iden Payne Theater and the Opera Lab Theater at UT Austin, and Synergy Studio.

The Deborah Hay Dance Company is a non-profit tax exempt organization based in Austin, Texas, since 1980. We are grateful for your generous contribution and will acknowledge your support with all due respect in the program for *Lamb, lamb, lamb, lamb, ...*

Sincerely,
Deborah Hay
Artistic Director/Deborah Hay Dance Company

■ In 1980, on the advice of several friends associated with the art world in Austin and New York, I form a nonprofit organization. After six years of grant applications, collaborations, board meetings, fund-raisers, budgets, incomparably meaningful relationships with dance company members Heloise Gold, Emily Burken, and

Diana Prechter, I realize that greater energy leaves the dance company office and practice space than returns to it. I let go of the dancers in 1985 and the general manager Sheri Goodman in 1986. I make a personal vow to simplify my life, my art, and the organization.

Now I negotiate performance and teaching gigs; I write press releases, calendar listings, public service announcements, thank you letters, requests for donations, newsletters; I hire tech people and find volunteers; I barter; I choreograph, teach, perform, write articles, produce, and my vow remains intact.■

I rent studio space for a nominal fee from the Dance Umbrella of Austin. In return Dance Umbrella becomes a co-sponsor of *Playing Awake '91*. Dance Umbrella's name appears with the Deborah Hay Dance Company on all workshop and performance promotion and publicity. Every day I imagine a studio of my own.

Every morning I arrive between 6 and 6:30 a.m., mop the floor with a damp towel, adjust the lights I buy to replace the studio fluorescents, set up the sound system I loan to Dance Umbrella on a semi-permanent basis, and cover the two wall-length mirrors with black velour curtains. I prepare the altar last.

Artificial air-circulation replaces windows and ventilation in the studio. At first we average two eight-inch tapered candles per day because the altar sits in the path of the blower fan. I move the altar to a quieter setting. A pair of candles now averages several days of dancing.

New objects appear on the altar: photographs of children and loved ones, a painted clay turtle whistle, a green stone anteater with hair growing from the ridge along its back, poems, candy.

As children we play hide and seek while lunch waits. Playing matters. As adults dancing together, remembering to play matters.

Nina Winthrop, a choreographer from New York who is participating in the workshop, offers to be responsible for the flowers. One week we have eight thick-stemmed white gladioli, gradually opening over the course of five days from tight laddered buds into soft fleshy trumpets. Prior to the gladioli she brings two thick bunches of daisies circled by fern.

"Some of you experience impermanence as limiting. What I mean by impermanence is not loss. What I mean by impermanence is a steadily transforming present. What I mean by seeing impermanence is a feeling of humility."

Each audience member is greeted individually and handed a program by one of several performers. A suggestion to "notice the inner activity of your stillness and impermanence" is made. These attributes are reflected in the shacks and the performers inside the shacks that fill the lobby ahead.

Everything is an apparition. *I am the impermanence I see.*

I position myself inside the front door of the lobby. My role amid the wave of people is overwhelming. I run backstage and summon a group of dancers to help me meet our audience.

I think part of the success of the workshop is its unique Texas location. The people who attend are usually students or teachers taking a semester off from school; artists, poets, dancers, performers, healers, replacing a northern winter without leaving their interest in discipline behind; individuals in a job transition with a window of opportunity to fulfill a childhood dream, some of whom have never danced and always wanted to, many of whom have never performed; people I meet in workshops or performance settings at colleges or alternative performance venues who recognize something that draws them to study with me. Additionally, Austin is one of the few remaining cities in America where it is possible to live well on relatively little money.

Prior to the public performances of *Lamb, lamb . . .* are two free public events called *Playing Audience*. While the workshop participants practice the performance meditation *I am the impermanence I see*, I sit with the audience and:
—read quotes from physicists, philosophers, and healers
—suggest alternative contexts for seeing movement
—encourage a dialogue among audience members about what they are experiencing.

The event runs for an hour. The first one is on St. Patrick's Day. The dancers decide to wear green or black.

According to the bootstrap hypothesis, nature cannot be reduced to fundamental entities, like fundamental building blocks of matter, but has to be understood entirely through self-consistency. Things exist by virtue of their mutually consistent relationships, and all of physics has to follow uniquely from the requirement that its components be consistent with one another and with themselves. "Carried to its logical extreme," writes Chew [the creator of the bootstrap hypothesis], "the bootstrap conjecture implies that the existence of consciousness, along with all other aspects of nature, is necessary for self-consistency of the whole."

According to Prigogine, physicist, chemist, and Nobel Laureate, the patterns of organizations characteristic of living systems can be summarized in terms of a single dynamic principle, the principle of self-organization. A living organism is a self-organizing system, which means that its order is not imposed by the environment but is established by the system itself. In other words, self-organizing systems exhibit a certain degree of autonomy. This does not mean that they are isolated from their environment; on the contrary, they interact with it continually, but this interaction does not determine their organization; they are self-organizing.—Fritjof Capra, *Uncommon Wisdom*

Mind is the essence of being alive.—Gregory Bateson

When I ask what brings people to the workshop, many reply "I want to be in my body more." For these dancers, my work serves to remind them that they are.

There is no selection process for the workshop. Aside from the fee, whoever is willing to commit to arriving on time to play awake for three hours daily for four months is welcome.

How is it that the moment I grasp the hands beside me and see a circle curving and across from where I stand, I am held holding everyone's hand?

Our circle is big, at other times small, despite the same number of people.

I deliberately use music to arouse heart energy that is often slow to rise from my culturally muted body. It is effortless to promote an enthusiasm for movement by playing tapes that are surprising and aesthetically stimulating. I have collected an extensive cassette library of indigenous peoples' music and a growing selection of works by new music composers. I find great pleasure, and undoubtedly a great sense of power, in placing my finger on PLAY.

People mill around and visit the various dwellings while sacred music is heard coming from inside the theater. It plays at a low volume so as not to intrude or shape the events in the lobby but to stimulate quietude and curiosity.

During a week-long stay in a Balinese mountain village in 1986, I first witness prayer performed within a daily ritual. Men, women, and children, whenever so moved, place flower petals and rice grain offerings on saucer-size palm leaves, leaving them wherever flat surfaces turn up. After preparing an offering, an individual gently bows the spine and head forward while both palms turn upward, the rotation and feeling in the hands expressing unmistakable surrender. The gesture is momentary but unfamiliar enough to stir a considerable wave of emotion several times a day when I happen to be present for it.

Surrounded on three sides by the group, I thank my mother, father, family, friends, and the greater and lesser powers which bring me to the first day of the workshop.

I thank my mother, whose stage name at the Roxy Theater is Shirley Redfield. From the age of four through twelve, she is my ballet, tap, musical comedy, and acrobatics teacher. She never asks if I want to dance.

I thank my father. While he is ballroom dancing with my mother, I watch anticipating the moment when he and I will assume the posture my mother taught us and we will gracefully begin circling the dance floor with my relatives, celebrating their weddings and Bar Mitzvahs.

I thank all the strange dance teachers, who, as immigrants and ordinary folk, are bold enough to teach advanced ballet and tap classes to thousands of young teenage girls, me being one of them, in housing projects and community centers throughout Brooklyn.

I thank Bill Frank, the first dance teacher I chose to study with because of his beautiful smile, ebony skin color, and his grand and eloquent style. I first study with him at the Henry Street Playhouse before following him from studio to studio for the next four years. He choreographs duets for us in addition to his solo and group dances. On Wednesday and Friday nights we go uptown to the Palladium on Broadway and 53rd Street and dance to Latin music until I catch the subway back to Brooklyn to meet my curfew. My parents are never aware of the hours I spend spinning, dipping, twirling around the crystal ballroom dancing the merengue, cha-cha-cha, rumba, samba, primarily with Bill, or if not, within his protective care.

I thank Merce Cunningham and Mia Slavenska for making me strong, cool, and qualified in my dancing.

I thank those artists, choreographers, composers, poets, and performers, who are driven, no matter how patiently, to tear apart, furrow through, suck dry, ignite, re-invent their respective art forms in order to create.

I thank Beverly Bajema for her uncompromising friendship and artistic generosity.

I thank everyone present for responding to whatever attracted you to join me this morning.

For the next hour everyone in turn gives thanks and bows. Almost everyone bows similarly. I am moved by the group's readiness to humble themselves. What I notice is the visibility of surrender in the upper spine just before the completion of the curve where the forehead meets the floor. Twenty-one-year-old Chris McCarthy, from Mad Brook Farm in Vermont, thanks his mother and the people at the farm for helping him get to the workshop. This touches me deeply because Mad Brook Farm, a community in northeastern Vermont, is my home from 1970 to 76. It is there that I give birth to my daughter Savannah; learn to garden and cultivate vegetables, flowers, and grains; let my body guide me; discover silence and other values that continue to influence my actions in the world.

A performer's inattention is glaringly visible. Questions rush in to fill the space where attention has been—whereas a performer's attention, without question, elicits audience attention.

At 8:10 the music ends, and the doors to the theater open. One remaining ball-shaped shack, woven from tightly curled crepe myrtle branches that are painted white, stands behind the seats in full view of the audience as they step into the soft light of the theater. Inside the myrtle igloo, a performer sits beside a candle in a clear glass dish. Some spectators notice the quiet pair. (Beverly Bajema made and inhabits this shack. She comes to *Lamb, lamb, lamb . . .* after participating in eleven of the twelve Austin-based large-group workshops that I have led. Tonight she is a model of the attention I seek. Although she is still, there is an abundance of ease, clarity, and scintillating interest about her body—she is a sister to the candle in the glass dish.) Most of the audience look toward their seats. Heleri and Brenda Cotto-Escalera are onstage opposite one another, twirling four-foot broomsticks wrapped with silver foil.

Open thou mine eyes, that I may behold wondrous things out of thy law. I am a stranger in the earth . . .
—Psalm 119:18-19

Seeing impermanence is not about scanning one's visual field. Seeing impermanence requires admitting that *nothing I see is forever.* From this perspective, wonders never cease.

Beverly gives me feedback in writing over the course of the workshop. It is her way to address details or noteworthy observations I miss:

—Make sure the new people get to give their thanks and bow.
—Are you still going to do sound at the beginning of class and prepare an ending so that we can take the work out into the world?
—Announce how I am going to be using after-class time. I plan to be available on Mondays from 5 to 6:30 p.m. at my house and Fridays, immediately following class, in the hall outside the studio. Everyone will have equal time to share their personal experience in the workshop.
—Who will maintain the altar?
—Who will pick up Heleri in the mornings? Have Heleri describe how she best hears everyone.
—Describe the Wednesday night class again. There is confusion about the appropriateness of other art forms and whether artists of all disciplines are welcome.

—Let's hear names again.

People are asked to provide a story, joke, or some exclamatory behavior to accompany their name. "Charissa, not chorizo. I was called chorizo all through grade school." "Brrrenda, I am from Puerrrrto Rrrico."

"I am Beverly Bajema, pronounced "Bye ma." I was born in 1951 and grew up on a dairy farm north of Bellingham, Washington. I supported myself as a housecleaner for twenty years until 1991. Since 1980 I have been a performance artist doing my own work and many collaborations. In 1987 I married Will Dibrell, a native Texan, a former auto mechanic, and more recently a lawyer.

Beverly Bajema holding Scott Heron during performance meditation practice.

"I am not a trained dancer. I am engaged in an eclectic movement exploration for my own pleasure and curiosity and as an enjoyable way to be close to other people.

"I met Deborah Hay in a gymnasium at Western Washington State College in Bellingham in the mid 1970s. She was touring with her *Ten Circle Dances* and her three-year-old daughter. Over the next few years I partook in over sixty evenings of Circle Dances with many of my friends, using Deborah's book, *Moving through the Universe in Bare Feet* (published by Swallow Press) as a guide. In the summer of 1979, I learned *The Grand Dance*, a three-hour performance ritual, in an outdoor workshop Deborah taught at Western Washington State College. She invited me to come to Austin to participate in her first large-group workshop *HEAVEN / below*, which I did.

"About midway through *HEAVEN / below* I tore my achilles tendon (not in the workshop). For two months I sat with Deborah and watched the daily performance of the piece. I observed details of the choreography from my own perspective as an untrained dancer and talked with Deborah about what I saw.

"After Deborah formed her dance company in 1980, she invited me to watch rehearsals for a week or two prior to each performance. Deborah was performing with her company, and I played the part of her eyes—from outside the dance—looking for ways to fine-tune the choreography and noting when my viewing attention wandered. I also traveled with the company—I watched and supported their performances, ironed costumes, and provided technical support.

"So far I have danced in thirteen of the large-group workshops which culminated in these performances:

HEAVEN / below (Spring 1980)
Heavily Laden Fruit (Fall 1980)
Grace (a selected group of nine women—1981)
Promenade (1982)
Movement of Light (1983)
Performance in Three Parts (1984)
Tasting the Blaze (1985)
The Love Song Project (1986)
The Navigator (1987)
The Gardener (1988)
Lamb, lamb, lamb . . . (1991)

I did not participate in the 1989 workshop *The Aviator.* In 1988 Deborah and I collaborated on an intimate performance event called *Living Room Duet.*

"Aside from my commitment to the practice of arriving on time and every day, I assist Deborah by playing a variety of differing roles. For example:

—I personify the most bizarre dancer.
—I am very openly affectionate with every dancer.
—I rest.
—I look for dancers who need help returning to the present moment and dance with them.
—I see what the group is doing and I do the opposite.
—I avoid any pretense that I know what Deborah's work is about.
—I give up caretaking roles and dance for myself.
—I set up discussion groups and support groups for the dancers.
—I take notes on Deborah's daily talks and choreographic instructions and relay them to dancers who are absent or late.

"I frequently invite dancers over for lunch to talk with them about the workshop and sometimes I host workshop-related parties. I have room in my home for out-of-town dancers to stay until they find homes.

"In 1990 four years after Deborah simplified her business, she asked me to be the contact person for the large-group workshop. I answer questions by phone and letter and mail materials on request.

"When new ideas, changing circumstances, and unusual or difficult situations arise in a workshop, Deborah often calls me and we listen to each other's thinking on the matter.

"In 1990 Deborah and I worked together to develop a support network for Austin performers who were developing their own work. We began the Wednesday Night Performance Class in 1991 that included workshop participants and other members of the Austin performance community. The class functioned as a venue to show works in progress to peers, a safe place to develop our skills in giving and asking for feedback, and an opportunity to talk about dance, produce shows, and discuss performance and production issues."

When I leave college after two years, it is because I realize my adeptness at memorization sells me short on understanding. I chose to forgo my copious talent but now find the scope of my accomplishment embarrassing. In order to prove that my capacity to remember is still intact if I want it to be, I learn the names of students as quickly as possible. By the second day I know everyone's name, although I am rarely certain of our number.

Guests are a new facet of the large-group workshop. Friends and family come for a day or two and participate with us. Charissa's eight-year-old daughter, Tiffin, dances with us regularly. Her sensibility and influence are an asset to the movement bank we draw from.

In Ubud I attend rehearsals of the most stylized Balinese music and dance. Dogs, chickens, children, and old folks sit nearby or on the stage, where complex patterns of movement are being rehearsed. The "audience" casually visit among themselves or exhibit a quiet interest in the musicians and dancers. My eyes dart among the performers to read reactions to villagers who stroll across stage and depart. Practice continues without a blemish of judgment in the gamelan-orchestrated, clove-scented evening air.

I would like to accommodate a similar learning atmosphere but cannot, yet. This is Texas, not Bali. There is no tradition for informality during study or practice. Americans have work to achieve.

Every day that there are guests in the workshop I struggle to understand how to include them.

The daily multiethnic presences of Sheelah, Manu, BJ, Marta, Brenda, and Namsik bring a new visual element to the large-group workshop. The older adults, Jean, Leila, Tim, Ginny, Heleri, Mary, and Tana subtly balance the hormonal power beating in the bodies of young Chris, Heather, Savannah, Eric, and Rosita.

Chris is uncontainable, bullish, devilishly dangerous yet not so. He quickly endears himself to most. There are a few women in particular who love taking him on in big sister/little brother play. His humor and forthrightness are engaging. He dryly interjects his opinions with as few words as possible.

Heleri and Chris are roommates. Their mutual care is obvious. Before his buddy arrives and establishes residency in the same apartment complex, Chris shops, keeps house, and often cooks for her. Heleri gives him breaks in the rent.

Heleri is teaching Brenda how to twirl a stick. (Heleri is a short, round, sweet-faced eighty-year-old trapeze artist, marathon walker, and mountain climber with a beautiful pair of legs. Brenda is from Puerto Rico and a theater history student at the University of Texas. Three weeks before moving into the theater, Brenda becomes ill with a rare inner-ear virus that keeps her bedridden. One of its more severe symptoms is vertigo. She wants to remain in the dance and asks to return as soon as she can to resume in whatever capacity she can best serve. She is present when we move into the theater on Monday, April 22. Before starting the first run-through, she and her close friend Marta Moncada approach me. Until this moment Marta has performed the stick-twirling opposite Heleri. Marta suggests that Brenda replace her in this opening duet. Since Brenda, by virtue of her lingering malaise, cannot dance in the rest of the piece, she is the appropriate one to demonstrate the lack of both attention and balance needed for the duet with Heleri. I am impressed with their thoughtfulness and politics. It is smart and theatrically

sound. Brenda's plump expansive body hampered by dizziness, queasy stomach, and long convalescence presents a naturally less articulate student—good at not learning twirling.)

"As an artist and choreographer I lean on your visibility because as you will notice in the weeks and months to come, there aren't fancy gymnastics or stringent movement requirements in the choreography. What I need is the malleability of *the all of you* at once."

For the first hour to hour and a half of the workshop there is no prescribed movement; one of several performance meditation practices guides the dancer in any and all combinations of movement play. The remainder of class is reserved for the development of the choreography.

March first is the entry deadline for a poster contest for *Lamb, lamb, lamb . . . .* The posters will appear on bulletin boards throughout Austin. Heleri wants to design the poster, but I decide on a more democratic process to determine the poster artist. Everyone is invited to submit entries. Heleri brings fabulously inventive lamb drawings every day for the next two weeks and leaves them on the altar. In this way she keeps us abreast of her talent. Needless to say, her competitors never appear. Heleri wins the contest and is presented with a potted flowering red lily at the ceremony to announce the winner.

Deborah Hay and Savannah Bradshaw present Heleri with a potted flowering red lily for winning the poster contest.

Heleri gives verbal and physical instructions to Brenda. The following is Heleri's own synopsis:

"I am to be the teacher, and Brenda, the kid. I am showing her how to twirl sticks. At first she is interested. I am to accompany my teaching with verbal directions —or anything I want to say. "It doesn't have to make sense." Then the lamb begins to lose interest and wanders off. I do not notice she is gone but keep on twirling awhile. All this time there is a spot-

light on me. As I twirl I have a hard time remembering I must not move out of the light. I must remember not to stop talking when I twirl, and not to stop twirling when I talk. And every night I do

not remember what I say the night before. So I have to think on my feet, or just let words come out. I worry about it. About all of it. I worry whether I can keep it up fifteen minutes, until I learn that will not be necessary. The audience will be kept in the lobby until all have gathered. It will be five or six minutes (that can seem like a long time). Once on

Heleri teaches Brenda Cotto-Escalera how to twirl a four-foot broomstick wrapped with silver foil.

the stage, and started, I forget all and remember everything— I am completely in every moment—completely busy—not a second to worry. When the audience laughs, as they sometimes do, this is food and drink to me! I could go on forever. But I don't. I think I have some sort of cue, but now I do not remember what it is."

Through my personal interactions with workshop participants I am reminded of the terror of performing. I tend to forget the frozen isolation I felt in front of audiences. From age twenty-eight to thirty-six I purposefully remove myself from the stage. While not performing I begin to allow imagination to thoroughly penetrate the constituency of my flesh, muscle, and bone marrow by turning my body into an infinity of tiny organs of perception. My curiosity about movement is not only aroused, it is mystified, broadened, and made acute.

Imagination helps move me through my terror as a performer. What is a performer's terror? *I will not be good enough; I will do something wrong; I will look terrible; I will forget what to do; no one will like me; no one will notice me; no one will understand.* Like sharks, fears circle the presumption that performance is a future event, even if it is seconds from now. To invite being seen playing awake within the vast terrain of my scintillating cellular body requires scrupulous monitoring of the whole body by the imagination. By necessity, thoughts occupied by fear, self-judgment, or judgment of others quickly vanish.

Brenda mimics Heleri twirling but is clearly uninterested. She eventually drops her stick and leaves the stage without warning. Heleri picks up Brenda's stick and continues her lesson as if Brenda is present. Her stories get confused; then she stops talking. She continues twirling dispassionately before she throws her sticks down. Black out.

How quickly I feel a person's absence without needing to check attendance. At first I feel plagued by a vague sense of loss. This in turn stimulates me to a greater level of attention in order to fill the individual's void.

We perform solos. Heleri dances at the same time as one of the trained dancers. Heleri barely moves. She falls to the floor, gets to her feet, falls again, like a kitten. The other dancer is relying on modern dance movement vocabulary, including the presentation of the self looking beyond and above the audience watching her. I have to force myself to watch the dancing next to the dance. Heleri is so real, attentive, playful, and serious. I tell Beverly later that Heleri's dance is precisely what attracts me as audience. Beverly says I am training people to see this way. I say, "If we took a vote, everyone would have to truthfully admit the attraction to Heleri." Beverly says, "Yes, but does everybody recognize their truth?"

I cannot identify the feeling of dying as a body process. The action of dying is without direction, momentum, gravity, or shape. I feel running or yearning but cannot identify a kinesthetic experience with dying. Dying is like seeing. I look at a diagram of how the eyeball works yet what does it really tell me about seeing?

Dying is our common denominator. Dying is always affecting our being yet few can describe the feeling its activity generates. Free from the seduction of a physical feeling of dying we are thus liberated from "doing" or "not doing" it. I am not talking about death or decay. As a movement artist I am examining dying, realizing I cannot associate a physical feeling with its uninterrupted action on my being. . . . Dying just "is."

"When you observe each other perform, are you aware of seeing the absence and presence of consciousness? Is it a myth that consciousness is visible? When you see the absence of consciousness are you thinking, 'At this moment I must remember to *play awake?'* Are you being reminded of the traps so you aren't their victim when it is your turn to perform?"

I notice where I am "on automatic." The more attention I bring to playing, the finer the gaps requiring my attention. Gaps do not cease; they demand greater acuity. I still unbind the unnoticed and rejoice in hair-splitting emergences after five years of practicing and performing my evening-length solo, *The Man Who Grew Common in Wisdom.*

The backdrop hangs in hundreds of tiny cloth pieces; orange extension cords make an inverted snake pit of the ceiling; dust, drabness, and a distinct feeling of loss and emptiness figure prominently in my experience when I enter the low-budget Vortex theater in the middle of the afternoon. John Job, who agrees to design and run the lights, meets me here. He paces while I talk with the theater owners, Bonnie and Steve, as if everything is fine, and in a way it is. I have been here before, so to speak, and know that vision, contemplation, cooperation, and enthusiasm can transform any arena into Theater.

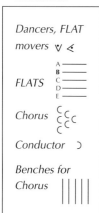

Key to illustrations

Dancers, FLAT movers ν ∡

FLATS
A ——
B ——
C ——
D ——
E ——

Chorus C C C C C C

Conductor ⊃

Benches for Chorus ||||

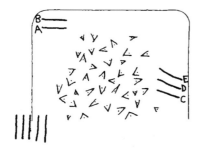

When the lights come up, the full cast (less a few) is sitting on the stage floor.

John does a beautiful job. He almost single-handedly turns the space into an intimate and provocative atmosphere although he has irritated, stung, and insulted beyond words Steve and Bonnie, who run the theater. Everyone is on tiptoe. His passion is enormous and misguided. His work is miraculous. When the performers arrive at the theater for the preview performance, they enter a clean, quiet, dimly lighted refuge for their preperformance energy.

The following happened one evening in the early 1970s, while I am under the influence of mescaline:

I am in a little room, a nine-by-twelve-foot tent-like enclosure within a very large barn in northern Vermont. It is the middle of winter and a heavily stoked wood stove warms the carpeted quarters. I think it looks like a Bedouin tent on evenings like this. The walls are made of reflective aluminum insulation, tree trunks, clear plastic, and fabric spreads. I live in this room with my daughter and her father for five years. Tonight I am alone.

A group of people suddenly appear standing in a circle by the wood stove. There is a leader—an old man in a tall pointed hat. Although I am seated in a lotus position on my bed, my psyche joins the circle and a great and perfect humming immediately ensues. I am held in this audible embrace until I feel myself begin to want to know what is happening. I feel my mind like fingers grabbing for an answer. The old man looks at me whimsically, points to the outside corner of his eye with his index finger, and tilts his head as bright sparks spring from the gesture and disappear. He gleefully indicates, "Lighten up, dear one." I relax back into the circle, the hum commences, and before I know it, my mind's fingers are grabbing for answers again.

It is not the point of the story to give up wanting. The point of the story is to remember to play.

What do I mean by *alignment is everywhere*? It is as though every cell in my body is hooked into a cosmic hose that grounds and elevates me simultaneously. Alignment in everything I see shifts my focus to include all of life intermeshing into one gigantic pattern of movement—and I merge in its dance. The only reason I do not have this experience all of the time is that my attention goes elsewhere.

Andrew St. Martin and Christina Morrison practicing inviting being seen living/dying.

Many people spend a lot of time on the floor during the first part of class. Culturally compared to a supine position, it is better to be on one's feet. I buy into the posture of standing on my own two feet since age fourteen, despite my body's appetite for being horizontal.

Eighteen feet above the stage floor are two recessed rectangular niches outlined

by scraps of black velour that fashion the backdrop. One cubicle, six feet high by eight feet wide, is placed center. It is brightly lit. Along its top edge is a hand-embroidered cloth runner that I brought from India in 1964. Six years later it frames the top edge of a window opposite my bed in a northern Vermont barn. On January 7, 1991, I tack it over the entrance to the workshop studio to bring color to a bland hallway. It is a surprise to look up and see it in its new context. Right of the center niche, also eighteen feet above the stage floor, is another illuminated rectangular enclosure, four feet high and eight feet wide.

Sometimes a dancer will arrive at 7 a.m. to help me prepare the studio for *Playing Awake*. It is an opportunity for a more personal interaction than is possible during class. We exchange feedback, I may suggest a temporary focus for practice, and/or we discuss difficulties with the work. The rest of the group begin arriving at 7:30 a.m.

I spend Mondays waking people from their weekend break.

Are you able to laugh at the seriousness of your attention—at the effort it takes to *play awake?*

(From here on, the stage is described from the perspective of the performer looking at the audience. To my left is stage left, and to my right is stage right. Downstage is toward and upstage is away from the audience.)

We sit bisecting the studio and facing one end. This becomes the stage area. I stand behind the group and direct what I want to see happen with the sparsity of movements accumulated thus far.

There are two areas of activity. Six people are in each area. Within the group of six one person is *on all fours moving without traveling.* The other five circle the kneeling body and *knead the air* with their arms and hands—a fuzzy nondescript activity. Behind them is a horizontal field of energy with eight or ten people who *sway to the right and sway to the left more or less in unison.* Behind them another group *has a good time displaying lots of energy.*

The movements do not necessitate being original, complex, or creative. The reduced choreographic stimulation hopefully increases the dancer's sensitivity to each passing moment.

Back to the group of five kneading over one on all fours, the fuzzy nondescript, and those having a good time behind the dancers swaying. I remove the people swaying while those having a good time are to continue as if the swaying field is still in front of them. Then I remove the one on all fours and four from the group of five. The scenario gets intriguing as we reduce the composition without lessening the original intent. To conclude, I ask the group to gradually build the scene back to its original number of performers.

Notes from Beverly:

—Practical matters: When people are speaking too softly, do you want to be the one who says to them, "Speak so the person farthest away can hear," or do you want me or all of us to be doing that?

—Cigarette smell comes into the studio whenever the Dance Umbrella office opens. It offends me. People are no longer smoking in the entry hall so that is better.

—Heleri called to suggest we have a bag of frozen peas in a freezer to apply to injuries. Is there a fridge?

—What if war starts on Wednesday? Will we cancel Wednesday night class in order to join the others surrounding the state capitol?

—Lydia had a horrible headache on Monday. She called me Monday afternoon.

—Loel is thinking of returning to San Francisco. She has the end of the week to decide. This is a confidence.

—I like not being distracted by food, water, or bathroom breaks.

I cry at the steering wheel on my drive to the studio. A bizarre brown-red atmosphere in predawn Austin colors my sense of hopelessness. My muscles clench in anger plus fatigue at men making war.

Every day the workshop starts discordantly. Living has a mixed and frenzied need to be realized. War twists our reference to *playing awake*. Does *playing awake* fail because the United States is at war in the Persian Gulf? It is so easy to appear miserable. We stand holding hands in a circle for a long time. The idea of playing awake feels selfish and indulgent. I begin to dance and the war inside ends.

Darling, you've got to keep revising downwards how much to expect.—Alan Gurganus, The Oldest Living Confederate Widow Tells All

Within the workshop the ultimate guide to one's well-being is one's self. No one is asked to strain or push beyond obvious physical limits. The whole body at once is the teacher of both limitation and capability. The assumption is that no harm is ever directed toward another dancer. With this understanding, participants are urged to surprise, interrupt, disrupt, and challenge each other's attention. Taking care of each other is not necessary.

Downstage right five rows of black benches face stage left. At the moment they are empty. During the performance one, some, but not all of the performers plus a conductor may be part of an ongoing, cast-changing, slapdash chorus. Upstage left, now empty, is the site for the second chorus of a few or many, with conductor, who stand in choral arrangement. This chorus may be partially obscured by flats serving as stage left wings. When an individual is not performing a sequence of movements onstage, or is not operating one of five flats, he or she becomes a member of either the sitting or standing chorus.

I want to use the voice as sound for the dance. Include your perception of dying in the experience of making sound. Each vocal moment lives and dies at once. One person produces a sound without planning it in advance. It is to be free of notes or content. The others listen to where the sound originates, how it is delivered, and where it travels. After identifying its instantaneous history, anyone may join in response. We hold hands in silence in a circle and someone proceeds to make an Om-like sound. I am sharply disappointed because *Om* is so obvious. I notice a similar discomfort in those of us more experienced in handling creative options. It is an effort not to interrupt.

A theatrical setting at one end of the studio, in place for performances by a group of Austin artists this weekend, becomes the stage for spontaneous movement scenarios played by three to five dancers at a time. The black wings, black floor, and spotlight are

the setting for playing performance now. This is our first opportunity to experience ourselves as audience. We have pressed

into, wrestled, stroked, embraced, and
grabbed at bodies that now, from a distance, stand clear and unparalleled. I
think, "It would be interesting to have six
or eight little playlets lining the walls of
the Vortex theater—each with its own set
of wings, its own story and chorus."

Note to myself: DH, go to Vortex and sit
in the theater.

*Sheelah Murthy,
Andrew Long, and
Heather Jarry during
performance medi-
tation practice.*

I ask Andrew Long to build five light-
weight four-by-eight-foot flats that can be easily transported back
and forth across stage. The labor is applied to his trade for workshop tuition. He is a young performance artist gifted in several
disciplines, one being his talent for building and construction. He
enjoys joking close to the edge of provoking alarm in his listeners.
A fierce inner dialogue is evident and influenced, I imagine, by his
New Jersey upbringing in a family of seven brothers.

The dancers have little energy for being a chorus. They forget to
sing. Halfway through a song, distinction vanishes. Some look
blank while others look to the nearest person for clues. I am not
clear about how, when, or where the chorus becomes the dance.
They reflect my inability to see them.

The dancers have the choice to appear with or without slippers or
dark ankle socks throughout *Lamb, lamb . . . .* Just after this
costume option is suggested, I read in a World War II novel by a
Jewish author that slippers symbolize readiness for death.

**The five flats are four-by-eight-foot foamcore boards with light-
weight frames glued onto one side for handling from behind, out
of view of the audience. A flat is wing, wall, or a transport that
brings or removes a performer from stage. Occasionally it acquires its own identity. Sometimes bare, slippered, or stocking
feet can be seen beneath the lower edge of a passing flat. As the
lights come up, two flats are wings upstage right and three are
downstage left wings.**

Spirit

Spirit is life

It flows thru the

death of me —

Gregory Corso,

Harold of the

Autochthonic

Ginny, age forty-nine, lies quietly curled against the wall with her eyes wide open following the movements of the class. She normally lives by herself in San Cristobal, New Mexico. On the altar, for just one morning, Ginny places her self-made cloth doll dressed in the same faded cottons and shaped into the same shy alertness that distinguishes its creator.

I am sitting on a platform watching the first part of class. Rosita is on her back looking up at me with tears in her eyes (she often cries in class), pointing to her feet. She is lying in this position a while. I smile at her until I see her mouth the words *I cannot move my legs.* I jump down, untie her moccasins and begin to rub her feet, shins, thighs, and hips. Feeling gradually returns to her legs while she tells me about her childhood in leg braces. She cries, agonized. I put the flats of her feet against my chest and tell her to push. Instinctively I feel in command of what she needs to assuage her fear and regain feeling. She presses her legs into me murmuring how good it feels. A half hour later she gets up and walks like a doe, choosing to watch the remainder of class.

John Job shows me his lighting plot. I innately trust him to get the work done simply and efficiently—two virtues that guide my personal and artistic life.

Suspended from fishing line above the stage area are ten white four-by-eight-foot quarter-inch thick foamcore flats that idle imperceptibly throughout the evening. The lights hang behind the backdrop and focus up onto the floating white panels, which then reflect a sense of luminous warmth back onto the stage. Combined with the five four-by-eight-foot vertical flats onstage, a coherent image for the whole performing area is created.

Delia calls late this afternoon. She isn't in class today. She and her husband fought through the night. She is forty-five and the mother of two teenagers. He will not pay for the workshop. He worries about money and she doesn't. She is upset. She cannot cover the tuition. I tell her to be there if money is going to be the only reason she cannot attend. She has the rest of her life to pay me back. With relief she says she will be in class tomorrow.

Four months of attention is guided to cellularly living each passing moment. Nothing is gained beyond the realization of an infinite process. One morning, like couples after a long separation, we return to the practice *alignment is everywhere.* The satisfaction of finally getting something, even as fundamentally basic as alignment everywhere throws the group into splendid heights.

Almost half the group fear Chris's energy. I tell about the man in almost every workshop who loves to skirt dangerously close to others—and how conscious that play must be performed in order to happen in the first place. Considering how often Chris flings himself through space, fractions away from the eyes and bodies of others, his record of injury is minimal. Persons with whom Chris is dancing want more recognition. He is not leaving room to be influenced by others. His strengths are blinding him. He relies heavily on his fast-paced snake-like changes, his cannonball alacrity—the drops, springs, and darts he perpetrates around others. The group is gentle, direct, and mixed in discussing their fear around this young man who seems without physical boundary. As the morning progresses, Chris joins many different people, and I watch him sensitively engage in partnering.

One morning, like couples after a long separation, we return to the practice alignment is everywhere.

Chris McCarthy and Christina Morrison.

Tim last participated in a large-group workshop in 1983. He was to that group what Chris is to *Playing Awake 1991*—except Tim was

forty-three and still challenging physical parameters. He returns to peformance after a seven-year hiatus during which he is audience for more dance concerts than anyone I know. He typicallly observes dance with his lead pencil scrambling across pages of loose paper or notebooks with weakened bindings. His dance writing is bizarre, musical, infantile, meager, humorous, and incisive.

Tim Hurst and Tana Christie.

Nancy [a performer from the *Playing Awake 1992* workshop]

Place a body
in a person
who that lives
across and out
its

Put a person
in a body that
can help only
live with
volcanic peace
of the lily.

A body that with
only a twist of hand
moves empty across
every where a leg
might want to go

A body not to surrender
but to give eyes
to sky never the less

A body that will not
surprise and then
will always
let go and
will say it wont.

That fades into
the openness without
the level of sincerity
that is actually there

Give a person a
body that clinches when
it cries and opens its
throat to cry leaves a
note of tear on the
next move.

Put a laugh in the body
and it lays down rolls
over rubs its nose
on the floor even if
it can.

Does "little" calling,
done. And goes
back to being itself
when it could have
been so much more

Until there is the
vulnerable on
the soft echoed tone
of chest allowing arms
to rise.
Lamb Lamb Lamb
is a matter of prize.
—Tim Hurst, 1992

I stop transcribing from the cassettes of my talks in class. My patience with listening to my own remarks is minimal. In a recent letter to a friend I discover a more introspective regard for the workshop:

> The result of being on the road for the last year and a half and using every opportunity to talk about the chemistry of the large-group workshop is most successful. Forty-two people are participating. It is a multicultural group, and this alone takes it to a new dimension visually and personally. There are

also six people over forty-five years of age. Their participation magnifies the sense of community. The unresolved anger and feelings of inadequacy, which we bring to the studio each day the Persian Gulf war continues, injects an air of abrasive poignancy into the practice. I keep up the good influence during the workshop, but Saturday, driving to the country, I sob clear to my destination. The more beautiful the day gets, the more I cry over the oil that spills into the ocean and our atmosphere blackened by fires.

In addition to choreographing the movement and consciousness, I am choreographing the sound (all human-voiced), and the use of lightweight movable flats that will swallow and unveil performers throughout the dance. I am passionately involved once again, and all isolated periods of darkness (which I thought might be hormonal) have disappeared in the enthusiasm for working with the large group again.

Returning is the motion of the Tao. Going far means returning.

—Lao Tzu

I leave home in the pouring rain. I absorb puddles of brown-yellow liquid from the studio floor into whatever cloth rags I find. Buckets are targets for the offensive drops that continue falling. The leaks add time to my morning's preparation. I hang black velour curtains over the two mirror-covered dance studio walls. I complete the altar, candles, incense, flowers, lights, and sound set-up just as the group begins arriving.

I announce that the outside door to the studio will be locked at 8:05 a.m. to reduce the threat of theft. As more people use the building more problems are being reported. But, too, dancers are starting to arrive late. I hope that the locked door will discourage lateness. The music's volume will neccesitate that latecomers pound on the door or wait in the hallway until the music ends in order to gain access to the studio.

Delia leaves Austin temporarily to live with her sister in Louisiana.

I hesitate to suggest ways to hold hands and stand in the circle. I want us to create our own directions from our own needs each morning. "Give yourself permission to get what you need from the circle."

Beverly's notes:
—BJ asked yesterday where is the lost-and-found and this morning without me relaying the message you have appeared with the

bag of lost-and-found items.

—I remember only a few interactions each day. I let go of them so thoroughly. I have never felt such fluidity in a workshop. Everyone dancing with everyone so much, so aware.

—I'm doing well at not taking care of people. Being equally available to everyone.

—I appreciated being able to come here and see the living in the dying after being with a friend's dead body last night.

Quietness pervades. Then one of eight Turkish names is called aloud: "Walat," "Vicay," "Beriman," "Hilin," "Recep," "Idris," "Meryem," "Sinan." [These names are printed on a blackboard by a group of Turkish children who watch classes I teach at the Center for New Dance Development in Arnhem, The Netherlands. The dance academy occupies the former site of the neighborhood primary school, which these children or their siblings once attended. The Center for New Dance Development recently opened, and the jet-eyed, streetwise children are extremely curious and aggressive about the lithe-bodied men and women streaming through the same hallways and rooms that once kept them confined. On several occasions, finding the children pressed and banging on the glass windows and doors, I invite them in to dance with us. The blackboard is the bridge by which we learn to speak their names.]

The Turkish name callers are:

—Namsik Kim, a heavily accented Korean-born male massage therapist,

—Andy St. Martin, an unbelievably handsome New Hampshire-bred aspiring artist,

—Julia Voland, a womanly midwesterner and former employee of a Texas state agency,

—Manu Bird Jobst, a young poet performer of Indonesian-German descent.

Manu Bird Jobst, Janna Buckmaster, and Eric Gould.

We did not come into this world. We came out of it, like buds out of branches and butterflies out of cocoons. We are a natural product of this earth, and if we turn out to be intelligent beings, then it can only be because we are fruits of an intelligent earth, which is nourished in its turn by an intelligent system of energy.—Lyall Watson, Gifts of Unknown Things

Forty-two dancers are on one side of the room crouched and curled on the floor. "You have ten minutes to cross the room without moving slowly." Almost everyone snakes and wriggles in constant motion. After five minutes I send them back. "Not moving slowly does not mean moving fast or moving constantly. I do not want to see squirming bodies. That is some other dance. I do not want to know what or who or where you are going. To know these things implies you are not *playing now.*" What I see next are forty-two individual entities instead of a river.

We practice singing the newly deconstructed version of "Mary Had a Little Lamb." Two groups stand ten-feet apart singing and gesturing back and forth to each other.

Three women are asked to lay head to foot, in a straight line facing the group. They are still although they can move if they want. The impermanence of the audience stimulates the sensation of their own mortality. The original chorus sings its deconstructed version of "Mary Had a Little Lamb" for the still trio. Tim stands close to the audience and performs *almost kneading.* He hears my request as *almost needing.* His face is trying to say something. I ask Liliana, the ancient, to stand with her back to Tim and perform *fast kneading.* She changes the scene into a vision.

Dying is ignored activity.

I cut blooms from the plum tree by the front porch before going to the studio. Tim and Eric prepare a sparse, masculine altar. Until this morning the kilim is spread flat. Tim and Eric fold and stack it angularly, making geometry with the altar rug for the first time.

On occasion, people leave the workshop for good. Nina does this after wrestling with leaving two times before today. Both times before, I encourage her to stay. My reasons for wanting her to remain in the workshop are varied, but mainly it is to support the continuity of the group relationship. I have no desire to discuss with everyone her reasons for leaving, although they understandably want to know why. "It is not you. The reasons are personal issues for Nina. She asks that I express her deep regret." I do not enjoy speaking for someone else. Self-doubt about commitment to the workshop abounds in many individuals for the next two weeks.

Scott Heron will present The Scott Heron Show this weekend. Many people in the workshop perform with him: Liz, Manu, Brett, Beverly, Julia, Andrew, and Namsik. Everyone is urged to attend.

Individually and without being seen by performer or audience, they call a Turkish name from changing locations in the theater. The stillness of the seated group shifts as heads turn away from the direction of the call or a name calls a dancer up from the floor and offstage.

Communion is experiencing everything, including myself, passing in present time.

Spontaneity disappears on request. This is more typical of the untrained performer who does not conceptualize the rarity of his or her individualism.

The choreography for *Lamb, lamb* . . . . is different from other large group dances. In previous ones performers are onstage throughout the piece. There are no exits. It is difficult to dance, exit, dance, and exit. "Even though there are exits, don't leave the dance."

I am angry. I have made far too many compromises with absence and lateness. I feel like I am sinking under the accumulation. I make an exception for my daughter, Savannah, by having her join the workshop almost two full months after it begins. Following her temporomandibular joint surgery in February, the workshop seems like the perfect opportunity for her to mend. I present the option to the group, and of course they agree to make room for the teacher's daughter. Lisa Foster, an actress and computer buff who has participated in several large-group workshops, is rehearsing for a show, rehearses way into the night, and is absent continually. BJ has a partial workshop scholarship but continues to find difficulty locating herself in the job market. Her latest job training has her committed to Mondays. Can I tell her to leave the workshop when she needs time to raise money for rent? I allow a landslide of exceptions and hate living with the results. It undermines the commitment made by those who have decidedly met the workshop prerequisite to be in class every day. I feel caught by my attachment to numbers of bodies.

Everyone except for seven dancers exits. The seven change from stillness into self-enveloped balls on the floor. It is impossible to read meaning into the movement of these physically bound, busy-moving figurations.

Movement in my dances inclines toward what is believed to be undance-like. Performance becomes an opportunity to air the rightness of all movement. The dancer's challenge is to *invite being seen perceiving no movement wrong, out of place, or out of character.*

I do not say that *alignment is everywhere* is true, although there is an exquisite appreciation of this perceptual experience in my cellular body.

When I notice workshop participants on the floor day after day, with the same movement aura hovering about their bodies, I lean toward becoming the destroyer, dancing deliberately close to their routine. I might stomp, race, throw myself into a movement frenzy near them. As teacher I actually spend much less time on the floor than I would like.

People appear less alive. Heavy hips situate on the floor. Bodies lean for support against walls and faces slacken. Eyes dart looking everywhere but out from the head. The few that have played devotedly seem exhausted with effort. I beg, plead, and scold, "I will not compromise you as participants in this dance. I have no desire to lessen or diminish your beauty. Without your rigorous attention there is nothing. There is no dance without you. It will not stand on its feet without the embodiment of the people performing it."

A palpable diminishment of attention ensues during the practice of the choreography of *Lamb, lamb, lamb, ...* "I selectively put limits on the movement territory you can cover in the dance. The movement meditation in the first half of class must be used to transcend the limits of the choreography or you will be starved for something to maintain your interest in this dance."

I learn that by developing simplicity, complexity is birthed.

Lisa Foster calls to say she is ready to return to the workshop. She has been in and out of class since day one. I say, "Don't. Not if you find it such a struggle. The workshop is already letting you go." Lisa says she wants to come back in a generous capacity. I know from past workshops that she has a lot of power. I say, "Lisa, if you want to come back and help me put this workshop back on its feet, I am more than willing." The conversation feels like the beginning of a turning point.

Chris is in prison, apprehended by two Federal agents with warrants for his arrest from Vermont. It is a complete surprise to everyone. Lisa's ex-husband is a criminal lawyer. She is on the phone getting help for Chris within minutes of the announcement in class. He will be in jail until he is extradited to Vermont. A judge in Vermont wants him there. Perhaps the judge understands how terrifying being incarcerated in Texas must be for a young Vermonter.

In one of many phone calls with Lisa about Chris this afternoon I say to her, "I didn't know how literally we needed your help in the workshop today."

Savannah Bradshaw and Heather Jarry, two twenty-year-old, long-limbed, kinky-haired beauties, enter jumping earthward with their girlish legs as the remainder of their attention mushrooms upward. As they jump, their hands billow toward their hips, eventually perching there. With each jump the sound *PANS*

Savannah Bradshaw and Heather Jarry enter jumping earthward upstage of the seven performers who curl busily without meaning. Marta Moncado and Eric Gould perform in niches above the stage. Conductor Liz Gans and standing chorus are stage left.

is shaped like petals of a flower and similarly set free in space from their unsprung female voices. Similarly fragile in countenance, they hardly appear to exist in gravity or duration. "PANS" is a breath spoken—not a word. It is the opposite of *snap* in every way. They travel upstage of the body-bound seven and exit relatively quickly.

All I can be at any moment is all of myself. If myself is more than fifty trillion cells in radical transformation every moment, I am off the hook of being any one entity. I am flux in a corporeal body. Responsibility to a singular identity is a misconception. Engaging the work of the imagination to translate "I am" into fifty trillion and more cells at once dispossesses fixed ideas from cultivated patterns that continue to determine what dance or dancer should be.

At age twenty Heather Jarry leaves a high-pressure, East Coast college to return home for self-evaluation before stepping out again. She signs up for *Playing Awake 1991* after one of the talks I offer to the community in December. On one hand Heather is quiet and retiring; on the other she is ingeniously playful, funny, and startling. This particular dualism endears her to many of us. This morning she faints among the seated gathering as I speak before class begins. I watch her eyes disappear inward and her eyelids slowly fan shut. Her spine folds into the shoulder of the person beside her. A gap is left where Heather was.

Savannah turns twenty on April 8th. At her request we have a garden party with an outdoor art exhibit on the front porch of our temporary living quarters. A gourmet pot-luck dinner follows and a slumber party gently ends the night. The people invited are primarily from the workshop.

Jerry Cunningham, a friend and advisory board member of the Deborah Hay Dance Company, comes to the party in the afternoon. He mentions hearing rumors that his house is a possibility for a postperformance party. I reply that I didn't think it would work because it is so far from town. He replies that it would be perfect because of the swimming pool, jacuzzi, sauna, hot tub, gardens, patio, and dance space. He offers to cover the cost of food. I listen, wondering about the role of party organizer. The work is unending, unless I turn the job over to someone else.

Seven bodies continue to *curl busily without meaning*. Their movement does not flow in an organic fashion. They are partnered at random by seven other dancers who enter and travel, undulate, wave, toss, press, and/or rub space more or less resembling one another. Each neighbors one of the balled-up dancers on the floor. The intent of each in the new group is to remove one wound-up busy body from stage without, for instance, an audience member realizing that that is what is happening. Jean Cornelius and Becky Fox (both women attorneys with exceptionally sculpted jawbones), the only prepaired duet in the group, exit last.

37

I look at the ceiling and see a dusty black, cotton-candy looking surface, trestles, light fixtures, and a skylight. I see a host of unpleasant matter. I know the ceiling will not be around forever, but I forget to remember this. My culture supports fixity. I forget to remember impermanence.

I change "ceiling" into "lifetime of ceiling." I practice remembering to see the impermanence. Separate parts start to disappear. Names vanish. Content goes. From here it is an easy jump to commune with the passing of all things. I am experiencing the death of separateness.

Becky Fox: "My husband is a cellular biologist at UT. He told me that we have over 3 trillion (3,000 billion) cells in our central nervous system alone."

Scott Heron and Chris confide that they do not use the performance meditation. It seems that few people do. In my mind this is the reason for the workshop. Nevertheless, I perceive Scott and Chris as *inviting being seen living and dying at once*, because that is what I am interested in examining about myself in relationship to the world, at this time.

Our hands pass from overhead, tracing the body's length earthward, drawing down into each body a clear, crystalline energy—a rarified frequency not usually assimilated into daily life. I can't believe I am doing this, an ex-New Yorker, born and raised in a middle-class Jewish suburb in Brooklyn. I think about all my artist friends and what they would say if they could see me now. The hands then summon the dark, rich, earthly, sensual, personal, lower forces of the universe upward through the body. We identify the inherent differences between the two energies. Several passings later, both energies are experienced at once—like riding a bike. One learns to manage the handlebars and the pedals simultaneously and here the ride begins. Experiencing oneself as the manifestation of the higher and lower *chakras* at once is a similar leap of faith. The heart-throbbing *fados* (popular songs) of Portugese singer Amelia Rodriguez sweep through the studio to further advance the momentum of the dance.

"I am addressing the artist in you. If that hasn't occurred to you by now, then I want to clarify. I am addressing the capacity to perceive that is yours and yours alone in the particular shapely way you perceive. For instance, how you perceive the experience of the higher and lower energies at once within you, this is the artist who I am addressing and whose visibility is being encouraged. I am not addressing a student of dance wanting to learn a way to move. My relationship to you is as an artist. The experience of your perception is the dance I want to see. How willing are you to reflect this artist—this continually changing intelligence in action?"

As the stage empties of duet activity, Marta steps into the center-stage enclosure, eighteen feet above the floor. With eyes casting about the performance below she is *witness and reflection* of all she sees or thinks she sees. Her movement registers in an effortless and most direct way. (Marta manifests as a gentle and virtuous being—dark eyes, very short black curly hair, a small nose, and rosebud lips. Her body is thin, lanky, undisturbed. She represents what we could all be if we weren't trying. At least she looks this way. I don't know what she is like to live with. As a friend said of *Lamb, lamb, lamb, lamb* . . . , "When I thought I didn't know what was going on I looked at Marta and understood. This happened without thinking.") She dances the witness throughout, including the bows taken at the end of the show.

The last day of the first week of the workshop Marta Moncada, from Panama, says, "All this week during class I have been reminded of something I had forgotten since childhood, and it is strange to be reminded of it from within the same culture I believed had robbed me of that innocence in the first place."

There is war at the same time my tears run as I dance *just so.* There is war because the body is abandoned—the altar unoccupied; a millennia of attention to invasion of foreign soil and minimal comprehension of the territory within. In this context it is possible to consider genocide. *Lamb at the altar* is the choice of the spirit to visibly inhabit the body.

There are many times in the course of a morning when I am experiencing several layers of reality at once. It is spacious and dream-like. At one point I am below Marta and her head is turning very slowly, her eyes do not see me, her head is looking up and taking in everything. I am seeing Marta's experience of seeing. Soon her eyes come around and at the last minute they catch and

gather up my seeing of her. She doesn't stop or dwell on me. Now I see myself being included in Marta's experience of seeing. I join the many realities she has already encompassed. She smiles faintly while her head continues turning, and there I am in her experience. I am with Marta and I am here changed and continuing my seeing of her.

*Workshop partici-
pants* invite being
seen admitting dying
in their living.

■Every year or so a new performance meditation helps me realign my relationship to choreography, dancing, performing, and teaching.

1986: *You* (you being the rest of the world, an audience, or a partner with whom I am dancing) *remind me of my wholeness changing.*

1987: *I invite being seen drawing wisdom from everything and remaining positionless about what wisdom is or looks like.*

1988: I imagine *every cell in my body has the potential to perceive action, resourcefulness, and cultivation at once.*

1989: *I invite being seen not being identifiable in my fabulously unique three-dimensional body.*

1990: *I am the impermanence I see.*

1991: *I invite being seen admitting dying in my living.*

1992: *Ah ha/nada, perceived inseparably.* ■

Eric Gould is in the stage left niche. He comes to the workshop from Wesleyan University, where he studied with me a year and a half ago. He just graduated with a degree in Cognitive Science. Eric is a dark, fluid, hairy, smart, languorous, intelligent young man. On both the first and third Sunday in March he is in motorcycle accidents. When he appears in class with a foot cast, Scott Heron (a young gay male performance artist; the realization of my wildest dreams) suggests I think of something special for Eric to do in *Lamb, lamb, lamb, lamb, lamb . . . .* so he doesn't feel left out during practice. It is not in my nature to invent special circumstances for the temporarily infirm. But I give Eric a cubicle

*Eric Gould during
a performance of
Lamb, lamb . . . .
Brett Vapnek and
Eric Gould.*

beside Marta and suggest he *exaggerate
the living/dying present in every movement,* **wringing it out of his flesh and
blood for an hour. He is completely inde-
pendent of the action below. In my mind
I see a madman. Instead he is a powerful,
lush, sensual, sinewy, gorgeously masculine Sankai Juku-like character in a white
jock strap. His choice of costume clari-
fies effortlessly what shorts and t-shirt
may have otherwise obscured.**

I explore the action of dying as a means to
expand my capabilities as a movement
artist. My brother Barry plays a pivotal
role in this dance. His poetry preys on
death. Only recently does my resistance
to his fascination abate. I place his new
manuscript on the dining-room table and
walk back to my studio. "Okay Deborah,
admit your cellular body knows dying." No sooner do I have the
thought than I am washed with a force like a deep, dark, rushing
river. I am pulled along by its constancy. I stay and stay in the
dance, alarmed, awed, humbled, breathless. I question whether I
have ever experienced living without the yardstick that dying now
represents.

I hear the hum of my body

perfectly still, my ear

pressed to the door jamb, buzzing,

the hiss of breath in my nose,

a distant voice that calls,

the knock and swoosh of plumbing

rising and falling through walls,

the thump of the heart, the slight

shake of the frame at the stroke,

the refrigerator gurgling

and grumbling tirelessly,

while I hold myself deathly still,

absent from house and body

and the music persists in its motions.

—Barry Goldensohn, *DANCE Music*

An impromptu group swarms onto the stage, hands generously cupped, fingertips lightly poised on each temple while the body motors forward *run/floating*. *Run/floating* breezily travels on and off the floor. The body is sent into the air by a minimally induced momentum from running. Some dancers exit immediately. Others take several more turns around the stage before leaving. Two women and one man are left *run/floating*. Eventually they gather upstage left and come to a *fake stop*. One leg swings around in front of the other, throwing the body into an easy but effective spin turn. Repeat several times with a *fake stop* midturn. The last turn culminates in an awkward make-believe freeze pose. A *freeze without freezing*, holding the moment in spirit but not form. They begin laughing aloud and both choruses join. Andy, the very handsome artist, jumps up and down with his legs apart, knees bent while turning around in a circle. His hands behave like fingers if his fingers were being used to count his laughter.

In all likelihood we will not see young and crashing Chris in the workshop again. I have known him, although not closely, for fifteen years. His history is troublemaking. I am surprised to learn of his enthusiasm for movement and performance—until he gets to Austin. He is focused, strong, and he loves to dance.

The day before his arrest, Chris arrives early to discuss his feelings of boredom with his dancing. Do I think he will adjust to four years of movement study abroad? He is naturally attached to exploring the edges of what he can accomplish physically. No matter how far anyone pushes, there is a two-minute maximum of movement possibility. I advise him to unravel the imaginative dimensions of his cellular prowess.

It is typical for me to enter the studio, lie on the floor, and fall into blind patterns of movement and stretching. This morning I decide the studio is the temple wherein my cellular body is embraced from light years away. I am touched by a million embraces before the thought is even complete. The immediacy of the feedback makes me laugh.

Our attention remains consistent while time races forward unconnected to the morning's dance. A collective "high" is being danced. When I have a noticeably good solo performance, the following evening I must bring a more meticulous relationship to each moment because a prior sense of satisfaction can numb me.

Faith is the substance of things hoped for, the evidence of what is not seen.

—Hebrews 11:1

Today is a practice dress performance. I suggest everyone wear something they love and like to be seen in, something that makes them feel good. I have in mind something pristine and relaxed although I neglect to say that to the group. I am surprised at how casually many dress. My impatience with the bland, free-floating, unironed costumes leaves me in bad favor with many.

I think about conducting a seven-month workshop. Following the large-group performances we would break for two weeks. A smaller group reconvenes, learning a distilled version of the large group's material. I savor this process as a soloist in the past. The group's reaction to my costume criticism feels so ridiculous that I wonder how I ever conceived of an idea like extending the workshop for even one day.

Tana Christie and Jean Cornelius, two professionally established middle-age women, lend an aura of humanity, as well as an element of fascination, to the look of the dance.

Jeannie McEwan, who is very straightforward and disarming, jumps up and down and from side to side, laughing and hand-counting. Stephanie Phillips, an accomplished musician, actress, and storyteller, hops while extending and dragging the toe of the other leg along the floor, counting her laughter on both open hands.

I think everyone is in class and announce it. We hug and cheer. Someone points out that Stephanie isn't here. We scream and cry. Stephanie arrives an hour late. We hug and cheer again. I think the need for a renewed commitment to the workshop does not need words.

Speaking confidentially to Beverly, I voice impatience with the monotony of Leila's dance. I rarely discuss the work of individuals who, for one reason or another, do not appear to be moving at the same pace as the rest. I trust they will shift when it is time. Today though, Leila's got talons! Is she affected by the break in form I share with Beverly yesterday?

Each of the three dancers leans back, reaches for the floor with one hand, and captures the body weight with the other. The torso is stretched open, navel to ceiling on all fours. A new trio enters _run/floating_, cupped fingers poised at the temples. This trio di-

vides to partner one of the bridged bodies. Generous, expansive, caring, stroking movement activity gathers over, around, beside, above, below, just off, and sometimes on the bridged partner. As this movement proceeds, flats E, D, and C at stage left progress on a diagonal path to upstage right, cleanly erasing the three

The torso is stretched open, navel to ceiling, on all fours. A partner strokes around, beside, above, and sometimes on the bridged dancer.

duets. At the same time, a chorus of five dancers enters walking in a line in front of flats E, D, and C. The flats stop when the most advanced edge reaches midstage. The chorus of five dancers turns to face the audience.

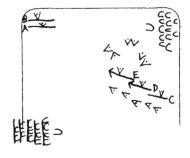

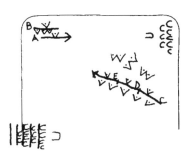

I am an isolated figure in a large studio; I am moving my body and I am partially awake; kind of exercising, kind of waiting for others to arrive. I stretch this and that, thinking of a few things to work on later. I am isolated in noticing these things about myself. One person arrives and goes to an opposite wall in the studio. What if I choose to perceive this dancer as a resource for my attention, energy to support my well-being? I do not dwell on her or think about what she is doing. I simply interpret the movement energy she transmits as impermanence (because this is the prescribed performance meditation for the workshop). This translation then stimulates the awareness of my impermanence. My cellular perception of her impermanent vitality expands to fill the distance between us. Instead of an isolated figure in the studio, I make every effort to maintain the relationship between us. There are forty-three other available resources at this moment who, without asking, multiply the dimension of my dance.

During the *run/floating* sequence, Beverly enters and exits *toe-o-ing* from upstage right along a straight path to center stage. *Toe-o-ing* is stepping onto one foot, stretching the other leg diagonally toward the floor without knowing when the big toe will land. Without anticipating or creating the moment, she cries *o* (the *o* from "snow") when contact between toe and stage is made. As light as a flea, the toe lifts and drops again, who knows when? The

step repeats; timing is personal. Beverly is seen exiting after the flats remove the three duets from view.

There is so little accumulated material. It is awkward to ask the dancers to try out movement still seemingly based in stupid action.

The movement practice is not about personal reverie. It is about playing awake

Beverly Bajema exits toe-o-ing as Jeannie McEwan, Stephanie Phillips, and Andrew St. Martin laugh and hand count.

with intelligence, curiosity, and the awareness of forty-five others likewise participating.

The group performs the short choreographed sequence of movements learned so far. I suggest that they oversee their adrenalin rush; the frenzy, the clever interpretation, the need to be different. I want to see the pure location of their attention as they dance.

I want to make a dance about stillness, without moving slowly.

Heleri appears as Beverly exits upstage right. She runs around. She is *barely the suggestion of a lamb looking for a Mary*. She plays close but does not succumb to imitation. She twitters and twirls, steps around and soon exits.

Playing awake makes reference to years of playing dead—as in childhood games and as tired adults.

Forsythia for the altar lies on the car seat beside me as I listen to National Public Radio and hear the timbre of war, the marketing of its worth, the deluge of its language. It is painful to share in the feelings of loss that then enter the studio with us. People sit quietly at the altar or immediately go and lie down. We begin playing awake, remembering the dance we have chosen to practice cooperatively. The room begins to take on warmth.

The areas of my body that may project less than the total person moving fill, as I imagine myself *whole and changing*.

We have our second and last *Playing Audience* performance at

Synergy Studio. Eighty people attend. I gather the following quotes to read to the audience during the event:

There is no piece of matter existing in a definite place that holds this word (rose) for you—it springs into existence from a region that simply knows how to organize matter and intelligence, mind and form. The atoms in your brain come and go, but the word *rose* does not disappear.

Subatomic particles are separated by huge gaps, making every atom more than 99.9% empty space. This holds true for hydrogen atoms in the air and carbon atoms in our cells. Therefore, everything solid, including our bodies, is proportionately as void as inter-galactic space.

Because we can change like quicksilver, the flowing quality of life is natural to us. The material body is a river of atoms, the mind is a river of thought, and what holds them together is a river of intelligence.

At the very instant that you think 'I am happy,' a chemical messenger translates your emotion, which has no solid existence whatever in the material world, into a bit of matter so perfectly attuned to your desire that literally every cell in your body learns of your happiness and joins in. The fact that you can instantly talk to 50 trillion cells in their own language is just as inexplicable as the moment when nature created the first photon out of empty space.—Deepak Chopra, M.D., *Quantum Healing*

Heleri and Deborah cavort in front of the Mary Chorus.

Twenty years ago I arrive at a cellular level of attention to the human body and I still turn to it for guidance. I can't stop looking into and out from this miraculous windfall of interest.

Meanwhile the five who enter in front of the flats, the Mary Chorus, stand with their backs up against the flat-formed diagonal wall. (Once the flat/wall is formed, the flat operators and dancers

may peak from behind it.) The Mary Chorus performs a sequence of sounds deconstructed from "Mary Had a Little Lamb."

Four weeks into the workshop and there is almost no choreographic material. I lean heavily on faith that the less there is, the more I have in terms of making a dance for forty-four human beings.

1. Sing the "Mare" from "Mary"; stop short of the "rr" sound. Sing "Mare" again after the first line of the rhyme is sung in the mind. Repeat several times. "Mare," a call, a care. "Mare," "Mare." Add "a" from "had" in ". . . had a little lamb." Sing it twice, . . . "a/a." Twist the head and neck to augment the "a/a." "Mare—mare—a/a, Mare-mare—a/a," without rhythm.

The sound circle remains uninteresting and egotistical. I hear an effort to be heard, creative, and/or different. Listening to people try to be unique first thing in the morning is hard to endure.

"When I am developing choreographic ideas I need unafraid, unembarrassed, and undiluted performances from you. This is a difficult request because myriad assumptions about dance, movement, and performance unconsciously get in the way. This is precisely why my choreographic demands are often ridiculous, illogical, and full of contradiction—it is to undermine what your body has learned, often without your knowing it, about the right and wrong ways to move and perform."

2. *Lamb, lamb, lamb, lamb,* an overly enunciated, thick-tongued, gentle utterance is created inside the mouth cavity. It does not land: rather, with hands poised in front of the lower lip, *lamb* is scooped back up into the mouth as it falls out. *Lamb* is spoken— not sung.

Thankheventz is an earthly expression of gratitude for the choice to play. *Thankheventz* the three dimensional body exists, whatever its limitations, because without it, the choice to play awake has nowhere to be.

My eyes read beyond the sum of forty-three moving bodies. Mortality and impermanence are the same. *Thankheventz* for the choice to sustain this metaphor.

3. *FLEESCH, FLEESCH* ("Its fleece was white as snow") explodes from behind the molars and runs forward along the inside of flaccidly vibrating cheeks. Pressing the ears forward as the sound is initiated helps keep it rolling.

Three guests are introduced as we stand in the circle. We have adopted visitor procedure. I am no longer ambivalent about seizing the time to coalesce the group and commit ourselves to a clear working order. After March 1, visitors will not be permitted to join the workshop.

Beverly Bajema and Scott Heron.

Scott Heron's presence is missed. I have known him since 1984 and value the continuing relationship we have as friend and teacher for each other. He is in New York performing this week. Everyone realizes his boundary-breaking effect in the workshop. He is a radical gay rights activist, a skinny queen, a brilliant performance artist with a heart like a jewel. Amidst his continuing and thorough exploration of the bizarre, I challenge him to admit his physical beauty and classical strength during brief duets we share in class. I do not let him off the hook with even a smile.

4. Sing the *o* from "white as snow"—a very short *o*—a tribute to every snowflake. Repeat often.

I am here, outside of time to know here.

The most distinct and appropriate feedback I receive is delivered when I dance alone.

5. Take the *LL* from "follow" and attach it to the *OO* from "school" in "It followed her to school . . . ." *LL* is expressed with the chin pressing forward and up. *OO* drops down to the bottom

of the inside of the mouth as the head slides down to the right shoulder. It peaks back to center with the chin, the *LL* sliding back down to *OO* on the left side. *LL-OO* is sung as a unit. Repeat often.

I put myself in situations where I am forced to survive. In 1970, toward the end of my habitation in New York, I share a loft on Spring Street and have regular opportunities to perform and teach; I leave to cohabit with people I have just met in northern Vermont. For eight out of twelve months almost no one in Vermont forsakes the hearth. Severe weather conditions and habits of rugged individualism keep people home. Former means of support are useless to me in this environment; however, I am experiencing epiphanies in perception which makes its way into language and reconstructs my thinking about dance. After six-and-a-half years in Vermont, I leave for Austin, Texas; a Brooklyn-bred experimental dancer, fresh from a Vermont commune, equipped only with a bag of imaginatively powered dance tricks.

I choose to survive with less. The same is true for the content, materials, and stimulation I turn to for dancing and making dances.

6. *One* from "school one day, school one day" is blown from the mouth. The breath from *one* thrusts the index finger (of either hand) forward in space from the lips. Or the breath from *one* is played transversely with the index finger wagging across and interrupting the line of fire. Repeat often.

I am dissatisfied with the chronological evolution of the dance material, so on individual filing cards I describe each separate movement learned so far. I take a moment to empty my mind and I shuffle the cards for a spontaneously determined order—even though many more changes will occur before this dance is completed. I thank composer John Cage for indirectly liberating me from taking myself too seriously.

7. *De* is from "school one day" without reaching the *ay*. It is spit from the front of the mouth, although it originates in the foot.

Stamp the foot to help get the sound on its journey up and out of the body. At the same time, with one hand at chest level, twist the wrist from facing down to up. It acts as the middleman between the foot and the mouth. *De, de, de* is sung in rapid progression.

Beverly's notes:
—Reiterate the need for people to speak loudly and clearly so that Heleri can hear without effort.

Excerpt of a letter from Heleri 9/29/91: One of the things occupying my mind recently is risk-taking. You might well have taken that as a workshop theme. Taking risks in order to live. You hear that some climbers are 'suicidal.'

From the audience, the choreographer enters looking for Heleri, *gaily doing nothing much*. She cavorts where Heleri just exited. Heleri prances back on stage to greet her. They run about. Choreographer (Mary) leads, dancer (Lamb) follows. Mary hops around the chorus, skirts behind the flats, flaps in and out of the wings, dances close to the audience, and turns to embrace Heleri several times. Mary joins the chorus. Lambs are not allowed in school. Heleri is shocked. She sits on the floor leaning back.

I mop the floor, set up the altar, hook up the sound system, and dance with people as they arrive. Announcements are made, a circle forms, silence, and I start the music while the circle is intact. It feels good to begin from a collective structure.

"When you are not on stage dancing, join a choral arrangement. I want the chorus to be in view and able to see the performers onstage."

I take Beverly's place in the dance. She takes notes on the performance. I love the interconnectedness of all of the parts to play in *Lamb, lamb* . . . . The options vivify my attention. I am chorus, flat mover, dancer, observer, conductor, let alone a river of moments.

Earlier in my life and career I considered being *just so* less than admirable. One of the more remarkable consequences in the practice of dying is the crucial realization that each moment is *just so*. There is no time to describe how beautiful or great something is if my attention is cast on this passing present—no time to dwell on feelings and thoughts. Everything I see becomes *just so* crucial to realize now.

There is a tremendous storm Thursday night through Friday morning. Big puddles lie yellowing the studio floor when I arrive in the morning. I do not have a shred of surplus energy. Our practice is lackluster and boring. So many people are absent. I speak of the hurt and aggravation I feel because of the absence of commitment on the part of many, plus my own delinquency in making so many compromises. I leave class.

Flat A moves one flat width toward stage left revealing Tim Hurst and Herb Pike supporting Sheri Goodman off the ground. Flat A resituates itself directly behind Flat B. Herb is in his thirties, tall, square, angular, masculine. Tim, fifty, is gray-haired, wiry, and delicate. Sheri is tiny and light as a feather. Without feeling the need to change position, or changing if need be, this trio is performed as is: two hold one off the floor. It is a trio wherein very little happens. They perform throughout the following trios dance.

Lisa Foster and Jeannie McEwan are seated chorus. Tim Hurst, Sheri Goodman, and Herb Pike perform two hold one off the floor.

Most of the time I have no awareness of a cellular level of activity in my body. The perception of such infinitely small movement is my lifetime practice.

I talk to Charly, and he claims that what he likes best about dance is the exposure of the dancer. I am coming to the conclusion that that is an illusion. The layers of consciously and unconsciously acquired movement-behavior veil trained and untrained dancers alike. The physical body standing before you has little to do with exposure. If you are talking about leotards or skin I am in agreement. But anything deeper is questionable.

In a telephone conversation with Bob Rauschenberg I describe *just so* with no doubt in my delivery of its universal attractiveness. He responds, breaking through my conviction with a breath of relativity, "Deborah, it all depends on the so, doesn't it? I mean, I am one so and you are another so."

Liliana Valenzuela, Liz Gans, and Linda Urton form sitting leaning back *trio.*

The Mary Chorus (five dancers), plus the three duets still behind the flats (six dancers), and thirteen others create eight sets of trios *sitting leaning back.* **A trio is two people sitting on the floor with hands resting on top of each thigh, thus rendering their arms useless. Their legs are outstretched toward the audience and their torsos lean back just enough to require the attention necessary to keep from falling over backward. The dancer stage right extends the left arm to rest, waist high, across the back of the performer beside her or him. The third dancer squats facing upstage, stage left of the** *sitting leaning back* **duet. The squatter's left hand rests on the left shoulder of the center figure in the trio.**

The trios form thusly: the first set of eight performers travels uninterruptedly and askew, a basic but irregular means of locomotion carrying them to a space that determines where each of the eight trios will eventually complete themselves. These first

eight people can choose to play any one of the three roles available in a trio.

Sit on the floor with both hands resting on top of the thighs, then lean back just enough to engage the whole body in not falling backward. This is hard to pull off either as choreography or as performance. Everything is against interest—the weight of the hips, the absence of stature, no additional movement directions, the nature of the effort. I know resistance to performing *sitting leaning back* everyday exists. This is precisely where the action is. It is you transforming assumption into an integrated performance experience for yourself. Reveal action from presumed nonaction like a magician pulls a rabbit from a hat.

"Forty-five people chose to meet three hours daily for four months in order to *play awake*. That is a radical shift away from normalcy. Do not waste time. Use the 8 a.m. threshold to be here ready to begin."

Dying, as a movement practice, is a step toward a nonthinking process. I bypass the desire to know by acknowledging that *wherever I am, dying is*. If the reflex to want to feel or understand dying kicks in, and it often does, I make a deliberate effort to speed up my movement, not think, toss my witness out in front of me, turn her toward me to include dying in what she sees.

I barely contain the bittersweetness of performing *inviting being seen just so*. I dance willing to die here. . . here. . . here.

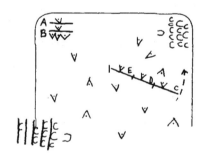

As the first group of eight take their positions, the diagonal wall made up of flats C, D, and E, alters. The outer corner of flat E is stationary, while the three flats as one surface fan upstage left, paralleling the audience.

Anyone onstage may sing "Tillie's song."

Now that the choruses have a score, a changing cast of conductors, and two designated areas onstage, they claim more interest than the dancing. The dancing is missing conviction. I am afraid I have worn the dancers thin with such limited movement demands.

The desire for private talks among friends during the workshop is a pattern. Couching it in important conversation is another pattern.

Beverly's notes:
—Thanks for asking people to speak louder.
—I have the feeling you are not getting the answers you want when you ask people to talk about their experiences. What is missing for you? The tie-in to the performance meditation?
—Our belongings are creeping around the corners of the studio.

[Tillie shares my daughter Savannah's hospital room in February 1991. At seventy-one, Tillie is in a hospital for the first time. The staff says she is mentally retarded. Until two years ago she lived with a mentally retarded sister, who died. Now she lives alone. She is impatient to get home after mild colon surgery. Tillie continually speaks sense and nonsense words to herself. Sitting with Savannah on the bed next to Tillie's, I cannot help listening, charmed by her jabber. The tone expresses enthusiasm for what is spoken and a real other person who listens and responds. Her talk is imbued with love. Chuckles, considerations, asides weave through her language. Real words jump out now and then. "Tillie's song" finds its way into the workshop's morning singing circle. Without divulging its origin, it becomes part of the choral vocabulary for Lamb, lamb, lamb . . . . "Tillie's song" sounds innocent until I give away its historical content a few days before the performances. The opportunity to play "mentally retarded" is pounced upon by the group. As it is finally realized in performance, I should have kept the origin of "Tillie's song" a secret.]

■ The performer of The Man Who Grew Common in Wisdom invites being seen drawing wisdom from everything, remaining positionless about the nature of wisdom. The performer maintains no attitude about what wisdom is or looks like. The description stimulates an imaginative field of action for the dancer. She becomes curious and alert about her cellular potential to perceive wisdom. She is relieved of attaching value to what she is performing. She has learned how to trick herself into feeling completely resourceful and fully alive. Her own personal experience is far too limiting to capture her attention like this does.

I perform *The Man Who Grew Common in Wisdom* at Bates Dance Festival in Lewiston, Maine, in August 1990. Following the concert is a question-and-answer period with the audience. Someone asks, "Do you think there is a difference between good and bad choreography?" It is a provoking question and takes a few days before I can answer. There is a difference between good and bad choreography. But whether there is a difference between great and awful choreography is another question.

For instance, I sit on a statewide dance panel reviewing videos of the work of choreographers who are applying for funds. Toward the end of a long session we watch a video in which several young, ample-bodied black women perform modern dancing. It makes a tremendous impression on me. Joy springs to my throat as I watch their innocence, commitment, and passion. Though the choreography is unimaginative, it is a vehicle for awakening the dancers and me.

On the other hand, I attend my first Bejart ballet. I dress to the hilt, take myself to dinner, and arrive at the performance early to watch the audience enter the concert hall. I am excited to see this legendary company with its gorgeous photographs and publicity. My seat is center orchestra. The ballet begins and I am immediately dumbfounded by the juxtaposition of images onstage. As it continues, I cannot make heads nor tails of what I am looking at. I chuckle at how refreshing it is not to have a clue about what is happening onstage although the people around me do not show signs of amusement. They appear to understand. Taking more notice of the dancers, I begin to feel disturbed. The women look rigid. Their shoulder, arm, and upper chest muscles are proportionately more developed than the rest of their bodies whereas the men are pointedly feminine. Feeding my growing discomfort is a thoughtlessly eclectic sequence of movements performed by dancers imprisoned by professional attitudes.

Bad choreography is the absence of a coherent aesthetic combined with inappropriate direction and training for the performers in a given dance.■

The desire to become unconscious is another kind of dying. The seduction to drift is so powerful that it takes everything in my power to remain present. "The desire to die to some level of reality is so profound that I need you to remind me to play awake now."

At the beginning of January 1991, I start preparing *The Man Who Grew Common In Wisdom* for a January 18 performance at the University of Texas at Dallas. For two weeks I complete Part One of the trilogy two minutes before the end of the music. I have no idea where the lost material is to be found. I deliberately stop practice for a few days. When I return, it is with the understanding that I do not have to use energy remembering the choreography. The two minutes re-emerge as I play *inviting being seen drawing wisdom from everything while remaining positionless about the nature of wisdom.* I have to forget what I have learned I must remember in order to dance *The Navigator,* Part One of the trilogy.

All we are is playing awake. No one here is permanently here.

The second group of eight dance their strange entrance, simply and without getting fixed on a character, finding a place within one of the eight sites established by the first person in the trio. Each chooses one of the two remaining trio parts to play.

Today I step out of dancing to watch groups and individuals, noting where I am aroused. Unlike sexual arousal, I am piqued by clumsy, slapstick, bizarre, plain, and daring movements and relationships.

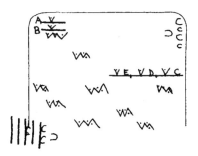

The last eight persons enter and complete each trio. Eight trios are each composed of two persons performing *sitting leaning back,* facing the audience, with a third squatting, facing upstage, stage left of the two recliners. Meanwhile "Tillie's song" increases dimension as the number of performers onstage increases.

"I am not your teacher. Your fifty trillion cells at once are your teacher. It is inconceivable to imagine what over fifty trillion cells will reveal from one moment to the next, but why not listen to this potential unfolding? The visibility of this intimacy is what constitutes the performance of your dance."

I want to provide just enough movement direction to ensure the visibility of the body's discovery of its infinite capacity to inform.

Seeing time and space continually altered by the physical and attentional activity of forty-four dancers reminds me of my own impermanence. To glimpse through this window to dying is to dive into communion.

During the first part of the morning practice I notice a pattern of going from one duet or trio to another so I practice dancing with everyone at once.

When all eight trios form, Eric *rings* the three cow bells hung from a corner of his cranny. The bells signal the dancers to rise and exit.

It is the last day for guests and eight join us. As they arrive, I notice Andy St. Martin getting tense and withdrawn. Just as class begins, he makes an abrupt departure and is gone for the day. I am upset because of the pressure I have instigated on the whole workshop by permitting guests in the first place. For some it is fun while others find the stretch a burden. I am caught in the middle.

We perform one-minute solos.

Scott Lehman is a performance artist who lives in Austin. In 1987 he is diagnosed as HIV positive. This year he takes a leave of absence from his job waiting tables at the Faculty Center at the University of Texas and joins the large-group workshop with support from a partial scholarship. Last night he shows a new work to the Wednesday night class. (Wednesday night class runs concurrent with *Playing Awake*. It serves artists in the large group and the community who are interested in creating and receiving feedback on their own work. During *Playing Awake 1991*, seven individual productions are launched as a result of this forum.)

In Scott's performance last night I see his fear of being seen by the group. It translates in the way he fixes his eyes upon us, pinning us to our seats. I attribute his gaze to mean "If I keep you there I will not have to deal with you here."

The summer following *Playing Awake 1991*, Scott again performs his dance *Exposure*. It is now more developed and succinct. It begins with him sitting on a plain chair to one side of the stage. A sound track of Beverly Bajema quietly playing on her accordion accompanies the dance. Scott is in the dark, wearing a white medical coat. His head is turned to the opposite side of the stage where lushly contrasted black and white slides unfold slowly. In each slide, Scott is in the process of tautly pulling the white medical coat from his flesh. When the slides end, the lights come up and Scott removes the straight coat from his very thin body. He stands facing the audience. Every hair, from head to toe, is shaved from his skin just prior to the performance. He dances like the petals of a rose, openly delicate and precise. I am being invited into a world that is barely human but splendidly alive. I have never seen dancing like this before.

The eight squatters assist the center sitter to stand. In an embrace they exit stage right, *a duet not knowing a way to dance.* Although facing and in physical contact, the partners carry their own weight. The remaining dancer exits facing diagonally upstage right. *Stepping backward without repetition or pattern,* a sensuous stage left exit wingward is made. Only the silent movement of flats C, D, and E remains on stage.

Chris phones Heleri from prison to say he meditates on the workshop each morning at 8 a.m. A few weeks later I receive this letter:

April 19, 1991

Dearest friends,

With you I had the best three months of my whole life. It sure was quite an experience for me. All my life I have always been Mister Touch, especially with my sisters. They would always get all worked up about me always having to touch them. So I must say that these months have been great for me by being able to really come into contact with other people that were more than willing to play with me. Now that I have had a big taste of this kind of play I know for sure that I will have to continue with it. I love the people that come with this dance. Everyone is really down to earth and friendly as all heaven.

It has been quite hard for me in here not having space to move or people to move with. I really miss all of you and wish we could do it all again. I still remember the very first day of the workshop with us sitting around in a circle telling who we were, where we came from and giving thanks to the people that made it possible for us to be there. I don't know about you all but I didn't know what to expect when I came to the workshop and was quite nervous. But after that first or second day I couldn't wait for the next day and the next.

I have some photocopies of pictures Christina sent me as well as the newspaper article hanging on my wall here. I sit and stare at them each day remembering exactly when some were taken and what followed.

I wish you all the best with the performance and want you to know that I will be there in mind and spirit. I also hope that you all will find something to keep you moving each day after this workshop is over.

I wish you all the Best and thank you for sharing the best part of my life so far with me. Lots of Leaps,

Chris
Del Valle Detention Center
Del Valle, Texas

Wherever you are, dying is is a trick used to short-circuit the deep attachments to thoughts and feelings about death. With practice, the linear thought, *wherever you are, dying is* shrinks to a dot. In other words, it becomes possible to reduce the image, which requires time and energy to produce, to a signal. *Wherever you are, dying is* equals *blip*.

■ In 1980 the dance that I choreograph for the first large-group workshop is *HEAVEN/below*. The dance is pieced together like a beaded necklace—sixty-four images, one after another from before the beginning through the bow at the end. *Leaving the house* is the preparatory image for the dance; other images include *short fat jumps, moving backward with difficulty, still summer hill, Indian dream fall, beautiful little animal dance, firm and gnarled trees, pushing and being pushed.*

Image operates like a fix every twenty seconds or so—a box of chocolate candies with a different liqueur inside each one. Over the course of ten years of choreography for the large-group workshop, I gradually reduce the number of images until the need for an image disappears altogether. What remains is a singular performance meditation to guide the dancer through the dance. The dances are more demanding now because there are no more chocolate candies.■

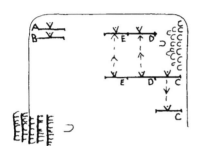

Flat C travels downstage and comes to a stop twelve feet from the audience. Flats D and E, their inner edge touching, retreat upstage, stopping six feet from the backdrop.

The workshop functions best when it is experienced as a network of forty-one interconnected whole parts.

Absences always bring my spirits down.

Until I have the privilege of working with twenty people in *Playing Awake 1992* I am not willing to admit that forty-two dancers is too great a responsibility—even with Beverly's assistance.

"Heleri, do you want to come closer so you can hear better?"

The stage fills rapidly. Running *hither and thither* is performed by anyone in addition to the nine who remain onstage after the others exit.

The desire to move smoothly and effortlessly, to gloss over simplicity and complexity alike in order to feel that one is dancing is as true for trained as for untrained dancers. Fred Astaire and Ginger Rogers are two flowing examples of dance who inadvertently condition our appreciation for nonflowing movement.

This workshop is not working as a laboratory for developing a new piece. Several reasons are becoming apparent:

—The practice of dying has no frills.

—All the participants are not onstage throughout the dance. When everyone is onstage all of the time, as is customary for my large group dances, there is no obvious time or space to diminish attention.

—Rarely do I choose some people over others to do selected movements. In this dance I have made many decisions about who performs when, causing feelings of competition, jealousy, and inadequacy to arise.

—People enroll to perform movement; not necessarily to be chorus and stagehand.

—The dancers experience little kinesthetic pleasure from the choreography.

Out of exasperation, I use five words—*the little brown stick dance* —to describe a movement that previously is without image to support it. I feel interest heighten immediately. At this moment I realize the severity of *Lamb, lamb, lamb, lamb, lamb . . . .* and the thirst to which I have driven the dancers.

[There are numerous traps in the performance of *hither and thither*. I watch the dancers struggle to discover how to live within the confinement of the form. An unsuspecting performer falls into looking lost, looking around, or losing definition. Eyes roll. People search. Blinded by quick changes and not seeing or choosing where the body is going along its fickled path are traps. The dancers interpret *hither and thither* as a state of mind rather than a movement direction. After the first two public performances I suggest performing *hither and thither* with the arms raised overhead, hands held waist-width apart. Immediately the automatic jogging stance, bent elbows, closed fists, hunched torso, disappear. Consciousness is raised with the help of the arms. Choreographing the distance between the hands expands and refines the attention further.]

Midway through the morning practice a spiral dance forms. Spiral dances seem to be a given in group dance activity and celebration. I participate and always see a few suffer the consequences of the particularly enthusiastic. Shoulder tendons pull, backs twist, and innocent people are dragged along the floor. When I feel one coming, I think, "Oh god, here we go again." This morning there are enough present who know to stop short of demise. "Maintain the peak above the bottoms of the feet. Do not oblige the crescendo of enthusiasm. Replace the old rise and fall with an ecstatic present."

Out of the *hither and thither,* three trios seemingly haphazard in occurrence develop separately onstage. The trio clasp hands and face the audience. *Passing to a prescribed other location with nonchalant care,* they step and lift a half-pointed foot, brushing it past the knee, step forward, and continue the movement on the other leg. *Heads are turned from the path* the trios travel. At the other location hands self-consciously drop and a paltry hula is danced. The chorus *starts to applaud. Starts to applaud* is the sound of enthusiastic clapping cut short. This signals the trios to exit as performed in the previous trio section; a pair from each trio exits stage right as *a duet not knowing a way to dance* in intimate contact while the remaining dancer *steps backward without repetition or pattern,* exiting voluptuously stage left.

As a matter of fact, those who maintain that they only enjoy music to the full with their eyes shut do not hear better than when they have them open, but the absence of visual distractions enables them to abandon themselves to the reveries induced by the lullaby of its sounds, and that is really what they prefer to the music itself.—Igor Stravinsky

For years "changing" is the metaphor for my attention to movement. Now I use "dying," taking advantage of the tremendous power, both mine and society's, of feelings associated with AIDS, war, famine, and ecological catastrophe. I seize the impact of fear and concern, temporarily lifting it from my head and heart. Activated by my imagination, I redistribute the energy from hard facts and emotional pressure into a bittersweet recognition of "dying" as perceived by every cell in my body. The effort to maintain this alternative awareness of dying is equal in intensity to the consuming negative energy from fearing death.

Flats E and D slide through space to stage right, uncovering a chorus line of dancers turning on their toes by crossing one leg in

63

front of the other then pivoting up and around. Weight hoists without lifting the shoulders. Arms stretch down and slightly apart from the body. The crossing leg and hoisted torso are performed meticulously. The performer is encouraged not to find a way to do the movement. Several turns are constructed in this manner.

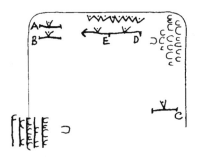

My unfitting movement combinations feel awkward and thankless to the person dancing them because there is no prescribed way to do them. "They are juxtaposed to inhibit your desire to learn them."

I spend twenty-two years learning how to dance, eager for training and inspired by my association with other dancers, choreographers, artists, and composers. Nagged by vague, persistent feelings of inadequacy, I spend the next twenty-two years unlearning how to dance. During this arduous unraveling, humility, dignity, humor, and gratitude surface in my movement.

At a party in 1963 I watch Robert Dunn practice his Tai Chi form and it impresses me. In 1965 I sign-up for classes at the Tai Chi Chuan Association on Canal Street, around the corner from my Howard Street loft. This is all I know of Tai Chi when I begin three years of training with Professor Cheng Man-Ching. In 1967, thoroughly disinterested in watching trained dancers moving, I decide to choreograph exclusively for untrained dancers, thereby eliminating myself from my dances. In 1971, my *Ten Circle Dances* eliminates the need for dance audience. Fear finally leaves my experience of performance as I have known it until now.

"I have no desire to impose myself on your fifty-trillion-cell teacher."

■ My solo repertory contains dances that remain alive because there is no space to drift in their execution. The choreography contains strategic tricks and performance traps which require ardent wakefulness or I am left in a sea of meaningless gestures. For example, when the audience enters the theater for *The Man Who*

Grew Common In Wisdom, the houselights and stage lights are on. My cue to enter is when I hear the soft opening sounds of Ellen Fullman's long-stringed instrument. The audience is usually talking, tricked by the presence of the houselights and unattuned to Fullman's quiet musical beginning. I enter from upstage and walk directly toward the audience and stop downstage. Audience and performer, in different ways, are abruptly brought into the dance.

Standing and facing the audience I listen for a short, loud bass tone that is played two minutes into the music. Integral to listening for the cue is not anticipating it so that when it arrives, without transition, I slide my whole body open, arms wide, the head and body sharply focused to my right. In a highly stylized-looking posture I take any number of exotic-looking steps diagonally upstage right. Reaching center stage I make a full but obscure turn before descending to the floor. Deliberately appearing to follow a formally choreographed ethic, I am in fact *imagining every cell in my body is inviting being seen perceiving wisdom while remaining positionless about what wisdom is or looks like.*■

"Two animals work for two days ahead of everyone else." Small groups perform this as spontaneous choreography. It is boring to watch. I dance it as a solo and only then realize the nature of my request. The value of the exercise is to surrender to and recognize the innate curiosity and intelligence of the cellular body. The story tells itself when I refrain from decision-making, interpretation, point of view, or need to demonstrate.

Operation Desert Storm is in the studio. The altar is noticeably simpler—one rock, one candle, one shell, one cup of water. I leave the music box in the storage carton. Everyone is quiet. Tension unloosens as we remember to *invite being seen whole and changing.*

The dancers begin *popping* downstage, remaining more or less on the same course—stepping forward on a bent leg as the same-sided arm swings open reveals the solar plexus. With each step the sound "pop" is produced to suggest the thrill of a burst sternum. Each step produces the exposure and expletive anew. Traveling downstage, the dancers keep the effort alive in full view of

the audience. With the trip complete, running *hither and thither* returns everyone to the original chorus line formation upstage.

For two days I watch the dance proceed from beginning to end without elasticity. It is too orderly. The performers need to engage in a sense of the whole dance at once; participating more selectively in their exits and entrances, chorus choices, and behind-the-scene activities.

I encourage everyone to take vast performance liberties and not to feel limited by the choreography. *Lamb, lamb, lamb, lamb . . . .* unfolds and I have no idea what I am looking at but find it fascinating. Photographer Phyllis Liedeker and I laugh ourselves useless.

Hands join as travel returns downstage performing the *shadow of a passé*, a relaxed foot passing across the inside of the knee, the leg vaguely opening forward before stepping. This continues, carrying the line closer to the audience. Two other movements are possible along this course: step forward onto one foot and lift the weight up at the same time the foot is placed down, or, the forward step achieved, drop the weight vertically, catching it in both knees. The lift or drop is made the moment the foot steps forward. The dancers slight the urge to figure it out.

"I ask you to perform foolish movement because foolish is an idea. Scott Heron: 'An idea or an ideal?'—especially about how the body looks but also how you think it feels."

Tim and his Andean flute, Stephanie/viola, Manu/recorder, Julia/flute, Heleri/whistle, Jean/drum, and Eric with a Yamaha electronic wind controller come together under my direction as composer/conductor. For forty minutes we play "Mary Had a Little Lamb" just like it would be played if we were adept. Then we play it incoherently. I enjoy conducting very much.

As this group nears the audience, performing one of the three movements described, another group emerges from behind to pass between and under their clasped hands. To avoid disturbing the ascent downstage, the new group *invites being seen crouched over and down, feet rubbing the floor* with no identifiable rhythm, pattern, or way. Staying short assures the original group's visibility as it returns upstage still holding hands, switching legs from front to back while jumping and landing with both feet at the same time. Once upstage, hands unclasp and each dancer exits *popping.*

One group, with hands clasped, performs the sha-dow of a passe on the way downstage. Another group in-vites being seen crouched over and down, feet rubbing the floor, without identifiable rhythm or pattern.

"I sometimes gravitate toward habitual patterns of movement and add a twist of illogic to the performance of them. Sometimes these movements cannot maintain the attention of the group. I will throw them out. I promise not to ask you to do anything that will humiliate or embarrass you. I am not here to make you feel foolish, unattractive, or less than a miracle."

Playing awake illuminates the body. Lipstick, bright trousers, running shoes, pale countenance, all disappear into the radiance of the whole person at once. In the absence of *playing awake*, partial images reappear.

The physical feeling of wholeness may be evidence of the presence of spirit in the body.

Toward the conclusion of the four months I come home exhausted every day. There is a pattern of fatigue perpetrated by my resistance to the mounting production pressures of every long-term workshop. I look drained and anxious. I looked so alive at the start.

Meanwhile the squatting foot-rubbers travel horizontally, facing the audience, to the left, right, left, right, across the downstage area. Behind them arrive another group, half-hidden, half-seen, *inviting being seen crouched over and down, feet rubbing the floor.* Everyone begins traveling upstage facing the audience, us-

ing the whole body to *draw attention* upstage with them. The intent is not to reveal the seduction. The original foot-rubbers *draw attention* clear upstage. At a choice moment, fingertips are placed onto the hips and the head is thrown back. Five light prancing steps, *pause,* five more, *pause,* five more, and so on, take the dancer from stage. The performer *sees;* with the head turned up, the eyes *see* a diagonally upward panorama while life bobs up and down from the weight changes of the prancing body.

Thought is captive energy in the head. It can be redirected from inside its well-protected enclosure so far from the feet. I take the linear thought "I don't know if this movement is right." I squeeze it into a blip, chop the blip into billions of photons

Performers draw attention *upstage with them without revealing the seduction.*

of energy, release and distribute "mind" into the body's farthest reaches, and notice this feeling is "awake."

We mold habitual facial expressions by earmarking ourselves as sensitive, innocent, impassioned, clown, or so forth. For example, I was a serious performer for many years.

Allow cellular suggestion into the face, the jaw, forehead, brow, inside the skull, inside the mouth and ears, the temples, the dark lip flesh, the bridge of the nose.

People are distracted and tired, part of the weekend-off syndrome. I begin to feel some *Is this all there is?* ricocheting around. "You forget the forty-one other individuals in this studio. The awareness of this relationship is a basic function of the workshop. It is possible to immediately shift into a sphere of attention greater than yourself. You can choose to be expanded by the vast amount of human energy in this room."

Every morning there are three or four people who invariably straggle into class after it starts. But the morning the video is scheduled for screening everyone is seated on the floor in front of the monitor at 7:30 a.m. I am shocked and have to laugh because the priority for diversity is so obvious and I don't like admitting it.

Each remaining foot-rubber chooses a spot to stop along the retreating path of seduction. With legs together, the arms stretch out parallel to each other in front of the body, drawing the torso forward. Next, the arms are drawn inward and the fingertips are placed onto the body, the choice and experience of landing clearly visible. The sequence places the fingertips lower on the body with each return from reaching until ten fingers stretch down, hanging just above the top of the feet under them. *Willing the hands through the tops of the feet* is performed briefly.

In American Indian or East Indian dancing, Balinese performance, Noh theater, Aboriginal dances, I feel I am witnessing the materialization of divine wealth.

Christina comes early to help prepare the studio. Talking to her I am reminded of the University of North Carolina/Greensboro summer workshop where we first meet. I admire the pleasure evident in her laughter as she dances. She isn't being funny but rather a whole person delighted. Remembering her then, I ask everyone today, "Are you able to laugh at the effort it takes to play awake?"

Many enter the dance as soon as the studio threshold is crossed. It is difficult to interrupt the individual focus in order to create a circle. The expectation of the circle adds to the units of attention already in place as workshop structure; individual time, circle, my opening remarks, performance meditation practice, choreography, chorus. Attention lessens in between each unit. This morning the dying practice flows uninterruptedly until five minutes after 11 a.m. I enjoy undermining assumptions about structure of any kind, especially structure I impose.

69

In tandem each dancer hums just enough notes from "Mary Had a Little Lamb" to not be decipherable from any one performer. Following the few notes, the torso springs back to vertical with arms stretched overhead. The skull immediately busies itself with movement in order to obfuscate the gradual descent of the hands from the air to the hips. With arms akimbo, the legs kick back and up, 1,2,3,4,5, *pause*/ 1,2,3,4,5 *pause*/, prancing beautifully with the chest arched and the chin poised. *Pause* is performed between each set of five kicks. *See* and prance, *pause*. In this precise and delicate fashion the stage empties.

Janna Buckmaster and Liz Gans: The skull immediately busies itself with movement in order to obfuscate the gradual descent of the hands from the air to the hips.

"The opportunity to materialize my faith in the unknown is the grist of my relationship to the workshop. You play a major role in my artistic process. It is not beneficial for me to feel judged by the very individuals I need to see performing. The only way I can see is if you clearly reflect back to me. You seem to neglect our daily living/dying performance meditation when we move on to the choreography. Rise to the occasion of living/dying within the most noxious itty bitty movement. It is a lot more challenging than languishing in the old time judge. Plus, when you play judge I get intimidated and scared and I don't want to use our precious time feeling this way."

Stage right flat D slowly advances stage left, depositing Namsik Kim about six feet into the space. An implacable Korean man is seen standing in a white Italian-cut t-shirt and shorts. Colored by his homeland accent, he intermittently calls out one of the Turkish names heard earlier in the evening—"Walat," "Vicay," "Beriman," "Hilin," "Recep," "Idris," "Meryem," "Sinan." When he calls, his head turns to

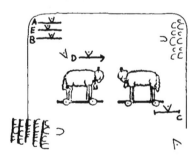

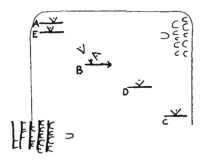

add suggestion to his action. Soon a tall, athletic, ponytailed Pennsylvania-born woman appears downstage left facing him. Slowly, precisely, and demurely, Ellen Waible, born in the same town as the zipper, advances. Stepping onto the right leg, she lifts and passes the left foot up the lower right leg to the knee, developing the foot forward in space before repeating on the other leg; she gradually diminishes the distance between them. The chorus is quiet. Only Namsik's cries (not directed at Ellen) are heard. A short distance before she reaches him, the chorus begins patting the floor with the flats of their feet. Flat B inconspicuously advances from stage right. At their threshold of contact, flat B passes in front of the pair, eliminating them from sight.

At their threshold of contact flat B passes in front of Namsik Kim and Ellen Waible.

If the body is an instrument for transcendence, why burden it with subject matter?

Because dance is where I live, I do not make things with it. I accumulate just enough structure to engage my curiosity and attention to continue to live.

"I am asking you to process in four months what has taken me twenty-two years. You are proceeding beautifully, yet you still create breaks in the workshop rhythm. No one here plays awake for three hours uninterruptedly, but the work is remembering to return to the potential for it."

Flat E makes a complete horizontal crossing to stage left, revealing Tim and Herb supporting Sheri off the ground in front of flat A. Without a change, or changing if need be, this trio is performed as before; two hold one off the floor; a trio wherein little happens. They continue through the following trios dance.

Beyond faith there is no way to play awake.

Meticulously oversee the performance of the choreographed movements. Notice where there is anticipation of the next movement. Then remove this interval so that intimacy is revived.

Eric clangs the cowbells on his perch in the niche. Eighteen individuals make their entrance onstage with an odd, uncharacteristic

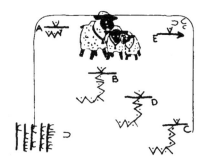

means of locomotion. Two sets of trios per flat form a right angle; one trio is a line attaching perpendicularly to the midpoint of flats B, D, or C; the other trio, another line, meets the person farthest from the flat to complete a right angle. Each trio repeats the *sitting leaning back* dance.

It is the first part of the morning practice. I lie in a pool of people on the floor. Big-boned Ellen lies on top of my spine. It is pressed hard and flat into the gray linoleum. My head can lift only enough to see bearded, bespectacled, art-movie-house manager Charly lying likewise, our heads at right angles. We could be on a Sunday picnic. Our fingers touch, resting on the floor along with ten other hands, a few feet, a knee. Once I see tall Herb's head cross the very top of my vision sailing before the background of the ceiling. Ten

Willing a right angle into a single straight line is played with as much subtlety as exaggeration.

minutes into this unimaginably perfect world I think, "An orgy can't hold a candle to this."

Later, I am arched forward into a bridge, hands on the floor, legs extended behind. I see Andy lying quietly watching off to my left.

He is my tent cord. He gradually rolls and scoots under my bridge, and I let myself down onto him playing *alignment is everywhere*. We stay that way for a long time. Then the flat of my foot touches his torso. I cannot see him although I experience his flesh, ribs, cartilage, the warmth of his intestines as part of me. I marvel at the information translated from his midriff through my foot. I lie crosswise over his belly, he facing up and me down. My arms are outstretched in front of me. The physical cross experienced as *alignment is everywhere* becomes a circle. He starts rolling, belly/back, belly/back, in the direction my head is facing, and I travel forward on my stomach along the floor, arms still outstretched, seeing the floor roll by under me.

When all trios are formed, everyone onstage, including the choruses, begins to *will each right angled-trio into a straight line* perpendicular to its corresponding flat. *Willing a right angle into a single straight line* is played with as much subtlety as exaggeration. Flats B, D, and C alter from individually supportive structures to one smooth diagonal wall starting from the downstage left corner of flat C and ending twelve feet later upstage right. Even flat A, upstage right, finds itself turned with its stage right

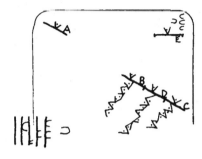

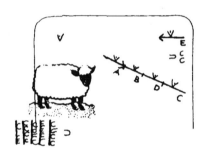

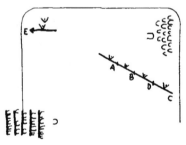

edge facing into the corner, thereby aligning itself with flats B, D, and C. Everyone wills the success of all transformations. As achievement is realized, the eighteen spent dancers release their energy and slip forward toward the audience.

Flat A drifts and attaches to flat B, revealing Julia, a plump, fair-skinned, arts enthusiast. (She volunteers her pickup truck and behind-the-scenes skills for numerous projects around town.) She performs *toe-o-ing* , singing *o* from "snow." *Toe-o-ing* is stepping onto one foot, stretching the other leg diagonally toward the floor without knowing when the big toe will land. Without anticipating or creating the moment, she cries "o," when contact between toe and stage is made. As light as a flea, the toe lifts and drops again, who knows when? Julia's toe-o-ing does not travel. Flat E crosses to upstage right, covering Julia just as she gets started.

We are audience for one another's solos, and a misconception about *inviting being seen* is clear. *Inviting being seen* is inappropriately translated into making eye contact with the audience. This partiality ignores the whole body's potential to *invite being seen.*

There is no music to lull the audience, no voice to produce reverie, no great props, set, or costumes. No Eurocentric state-supported art experience is being mounted here. The choreography is a bare wire stretched to balance the attention of the performer. It is secured with adjustable but finite movement directions for foothold. Along this wire the dancer juggles the art of living and dying at once.

Willing a right angle into a single straight line, *April 19, 1991.*

Flats A, B, D, and C, *float* diagonally upstage right, Flat A *attaching* itself precisely at the 130-degree angle it meets Flat E. A small

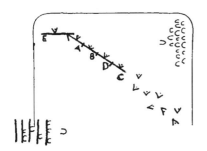

group of dancers is exposed downstage left in the wake of the flats. They perform mock robot movements. All changes originate in their joints. Their challenge is to avoid becoming machine-like. They travel downstage left, fading into the sightlines.

Tom Giebink calls to say the video he shot during the morning practice has a glitch and nothing can be saved. Can we do it again and when? Tonight's preview performance becomes a video performance. John is upset when he learns the preview is now a video shoot and not the opportunity he hopes for the benefit of the group. His sincerity in this regard is clearly apparent. He wants the group to have the warmth of a preview to move them into the next four performances, especially for those who have never performed before. To shoot the video during the preview also destroys John's only opportunity to see his lighting design. The wattage necessary for the cameras will wash out the evidence of his work. He rants and raves at Tom. I explain the situation to the group. They express support for John and Tom. The dancers' energy is so expansive that they will cooperate with any decision.

After the preview Tom informs me the cameras did not work for the first ten minutes. John walks out of the theater. The group is generous and we re-shoot the first fifteen minutes of the show.

The dancers then retire to Liliana's house. Liliana Valenzuela is an anthropologist from Mexico City. Her dancing is steeped in culture and authority. A sauna awaits us in her backyard. Following the sauna, our bodies flatten to the marginal surface of her daughter Sophia's plastic swimming pool, taking full advantage of the cool stabilizing water. Savannah drives me home because my exhaustion is overwhelming.

Flats A, B, D, and C rotate to face the audience directly. A split opens between flats B and D, revealing Brett Vapnek, an innovative and sophisticated twenty-year-old performance artist, and whomever else will partner her. [Brenda is Brett's partner since February, until her inner ear virus defeats her in April. With Brenda bedridden I decide not to assign another partner for Brett and see what happens within the group if I simply refrain from administering form.]

We work with partners because many people are tired. An undeniable birth of attention arises from the conjunction of physical contact and the performance meditation *you remind me of my wholeness changing.*

Brett lends me her video camera, and I concentrate on close-ups of the dancers for performance feedback. I cannot see the dance and what I do see through the camera is disheartening. The performers become evasive and self-conscious as I approach them. They are not used to the camera, nor am I. To invite being seen from eight feet away by a round plastic lens is a far cry from inviting being seen by a whole human being.

When my daughter kisses me on the neck, I instinctively lower my chin to protect the acute sensitivity I experience there. I absolutely forget how safe and wonderful it is to be in her presence. Perhaps the camera stimulates a similar act of self-preservation in the body. There are indigenous people who believe that to be photographed is to be robbed of the soul. When I look at myself on video, I see more of what is missing than what is apparently there.

Savannah Bradshaw and Deborah Hay.

Members of Liz Lerman's Dance Exchange join us for a few days. It is the first time since the large-group workshop began in 1980 that members of a visiting dance company attend. Liz's philosophy is to realize multiple avenues of access into community. Asking questions is the most obvious. "May my company attend your workshop while we are in Austin?" It is wonderful for us to accommodate four absolutely fine dancers. Having rolled in each other's arms contributes to our appreciation of their performance. It is apparent that members of the workshop are pleased that Liz's dancers feel challenged working with our material.

I post *Lamb, lamb, lamb, lamb . . .* flyers and then meet with Steve Bacher and Bonnie Cullum at the Vortex Performance Cafe to go over details for the use of the theater. We are fortunate to have three days and nights in the theater before the public performances.

I withdraw from my role as guide several weeks before the public performances. I end the litany of verbal suggestions for remembering to play awake that accompanies every three hour practice. "It is your turn to take the responsibility for remembering to play." I very nearly stop seeing the performers in order to tuck, dart, and in some cases remove the loose or ineffective material that interferes with the shape of the dance.

Before each public performance I whisper a new set of instructions to Brett to color the movement sequence and affect the nature of the duet. The following is a description of the duet's last performance.

Brett is a seething raving animal. She swells with growls and groans. Brenda, Brett's original partner for the duet, performs with her for the first time in over a month. I whisper to Brenda to be nice to Brett during the duet. Brenda is nice and Brett growls, baring her teeth and clawing her hands. Their movement sequence is performed simultaneously.

Brenda and Brett will their fingertips through the tops of their feet. Brett Vapnek and Brenda Cotto-Escalera return fingertips to a meticulously chosen place on the body.

Savannah and I are invited to breakfast with Brett and her family, who have flown in from California to see their daughter perform in *Lamb* . . . . I lavish praise and genuine enthusiasm for Brett's talents as a performance artist.

They stand next to each other, bent forward and down, *fingertips willed through the tops of the feet.* From this position the arms stretch forward, parallel, drawing the torso forward. The head stretches up and arches back as the fingertips return to a meticulously chosen place on an ascending journey up the front of the body. By the time the dancers' legs have straightened, their hands have traveled in intermittent steps to finally touch upon the temples, sending the duet into instantaneous *run/floating.* Brenda exits quickly. Brett circles, circles, and circles the stage. Each night I tell her to circle longer. She growls, moans, loses definition, and leaves the stage.

Our bodies ape each other unthinkingly. While speaking with a perfect stranger I might note a recurring hand gesture and an hour later look down at that same gesture being played as if it were mine. It is natural to be influenced by other people's movements. However, as a teacher I do not demonstrate movement because of how quickly others learn to do "what is right."

Excerpt of a letter from Brett 6/9/1991:

Deborah, It was a joy to receive your letter and to read the description of the performance. When I think back on that section I always remember the chaos behind the flats before they split open to reveal us. The flat operators never seemed quite sure which direction they were supposed to go and when. There were always at least three extra people who were just left behind the flats serving no purpose, just waiting to exit. (Then most of the time I didn't know who my partner would be, so I would usually be frantically negotiating before the flats opened.) It was always a time in which I would look at Liz, a flat operator, and we would laugh at how out of control that moment always felt, laugh in disbelief that everyone could be so frantic over something so arbitrary. Once the flats finally split I felt like a sky diver who had suddenly leapt off a plane to find herself sailing through midair.

"What a relief,"
the body speaks.
"No need ignore
dying anymore,
or dance perma-
nence."—D. Hay

The other thing that stands out is the questioning insanity with which (as the wild animal especially) I ran around the circle. It was a striking moment for me, because as I ran I saw audience, performers, blank space, performers, audience, performers . . . and I was just there, with no answers at all, running in that fucking circle.

As the duet unfolds, a group of ten or more dancers enters upstage left. Traveling to and exiting upstage right, they blow *one* (from "one day" in "Mary Had a Little Lamb") from the mouth

onto a pointed index finger held in front of the lips. Breath sends the finger forward or the finger wags back and forth across the stream of air, creating an audible interference pattern. The upper body is bent forward while feet explore space just above ground level. Forward steps are taken between their flush-footed exploration. They exit before Brett who is running like an animal.

When we *invite being seen realizing the sacred and profane at once*, I see everyone as archetypes. The dancers are momentarily nothing less than deities. I sense an air of absolutism in our company together. In contrast, when my performance meditation drifts, and is replaced by thoughts, self-conscious identity and lassitude reenter my vision. When I choose to read this as the sacred and profane at once, I truly fall in love with humanity.

The realm of the cellular body is inexplicably forthright. The expansion my dance acquires through enlisting the cellular body is second only to the microcosm discovered in overseeing the performance of it.

I sometimes practice playing awake outside the studio setting. "When does it end?" I have less control over when it ends than when I choose to begin.

Nine dancers shoot onstage performing combination step/ leap/jump/flash kick forward. *The torso* pushes forward/jerks back, both at once.

I listen to a friend tell a story. I believe I am attentive. Just to check, I say to myself, "Play awake, because I am dying." My friend's words get clearer. My body changes with the story as it is being told. Warmth rises and encircles my friend and me. Beliefs about what attention is or what it looks like need regular provocation from me.

Upstage right nine performers shoot onto stage. One and then another perform *combination step/leap/jump/flash kick forward.* **The torso** *pushes forward/jerks back, both at once.* **The torso remains more or less vertical during** *push forward/jerk back, both at once.* **Another combination** *step/leap/jump/flash kick forward,* **always faces stage left. The en-**

trance is ungainly but contained. Its wildness dwells in the presence of remembered movement physically abandoned months ago. The arms and hands were once alarmingly busy and inventive in front of the performer's body during *combination step/ leap/jump/flash kick forward* and *push forward/jerk back, both at once.* The remembered energy now suffices. Timing is not slow or constant.

Nothing attracts the dancer to the dance more than splitting the regulated and insulated currents of kinesthesis into myriad fiery lifetimes all at once before dying.

The stage is crossed. Everyone faces forward in unison, agitating the hands, palms facing but not meeting but beating in and out. Rhythm almost looks possible. Meanwhile the group is creating a v-formation, its apex downstage center. This spatial relationship is accomplished as one leg shoots to the side then crosses way over in front of the other. *Kick out/cross over, change legs, kick out/cross over, change legs,* etc.

Admitting the constancy of dying relieves me of trying to identify it. I am free to appreciate a crucial present, throughout my body at once, before it passes.

The next unison change is *slice open from head to foot down the center of the body.* Arms and one leg splay. Blow the word *fleesch* from between the inside of the cheek lining and the outside of the molars, teeth clenched and bared.

The question arises, "Do you have an image for this movement?" I do not want to shape exploration with a pre-existing road. The body is a curiosity-seeker if given half a chance. An articulate consciousness combined with undecipherable movement greatly inspires me as a teacher, performer, choreographer, and audience member.

The performers shift their attention to *flatly patting the floor with their feet,* legs spread easily and evenly from the hips. Arms curve

upward, balanced on either side of the body.

We proceed through the sequence from mid-dance to conclusion with all five flats. I am elated. There is a lot to look at and nothing to understand.

When the group senses its collective energy, they *lock butt* into place, firing the body forward downstage left then upstage right. They remain on the tips of the feet, keeping their buttocks fixed. They shoot forward, taking tiny rushing steps along the floor. They fall backward upright, making tiny steps, nearly beyond the balls of the feet. *Lock butt* is performed in unison v-formation.

The last thing I want to do is demonstrate how to do a movement because then I have to look at others do my demonstration. The transference of the demonstration is immediate, invisible, unconscious, and so subtle that it remains unknown to the observer of the demonstration. It then requires ten times more energy to unlearn movement not recognized as learned.

Any of the nine performers may start *snap*. Hardly leaving the floor, they jump down, snap the fingers and cry, "snap." The goal is to get each *snap* over with as quickly as possible. *Snap, snap,* facing the audience traveling backward upstage right, individually but as a group more or less. Arriving upstage, the dancers stop dancing and stand quietly as the head turns to look around. Eventually everyone stands facing stage right.

Becky Fox (one of the two female attorneys in the workshop): "Isn't it true that if, at some level, one cannot acknowledge that one is in some way dying at every moment, then one is already dead to some aspect of being? Simply put, If you don't know you're dying, you're already dead."

"Monitor the eyes. When they fix in their sockets it is an indication that the mind is somewhere else, not part of an ongoing, self-consistent, self-organizing system."

I use my eyes to work on my behalf, just as I use other parts of my body. When my eyes stare, I reactivate them. I imagine that what I see enriches me, and my eyes immediately feel silky and moist and what I see loses meaning and gains energy.

A performer's eyes reveal partial attention when they: fix inside the head, looking inward; stare out into a void; look up and out, inferring another reality; become veiled by the eyelids.

I spend twenty-five years dancing with my eyelids half open. "Open the eyelids from the temples. Energy will rise up and out through the top of the head. Maybe you too will salivate."

The person closest to stage right is leader. The movement is *skip/ jump backward and down* landing with both feet at once. Attention is in landing and removing all signals that initiate the *skip/ jump backward and down*. As the first person skips/lands, all skip/land. There is no beat. The goal is to achieve simultaneity. Any dancer may move to the front of the group if he or she has an urge to revolutionize leadership. A jagged, irregular exit traveling backward across stage to upstage left is danced by the nine performers.

Five men travel backwards. Their arms wave come here, *but the content is lacking in the gesture.*

Continuity of attention requires dying to the continuity of inattention. *Invite being seen dying to the continuity of inattention.*

Five men travel backward, passing slowly from upstage left to downstage right, with intermittent steps. Their arms wave *come here*, but content is lacking in the gesture. *Come here* is played broadly.

My earliest childhood memories of movement are: watching Larry the janitor as he silently polishes the brass fixtures and dark woodwork in our apartment house lobby; a rear view of big aunt Anna at her kitchen counter making egg noodles for Sabbath dinner; leaning into a dark basement doorway to a storage room with cast-off furniture from six stories of family apartments, watching my father, who after teaching school all day, refinishes furniture for our family and the neighbors; being entranced by May, the brown-skinned woman who helps my mother clean house once a week. As she waxes, I sit on the couch a few feet from her kneeling body as it makes rhythmic circles above our speckled linoleum floor. In retrospect, I think the compelling strength of these memories comes from the warmth and intelligence that emanate from their working bodies.

Dance uses the limitation of the physical body to expand the quality of attention one brings to the world. At its peak it defractionalizes the moment for the dancer and the audience.

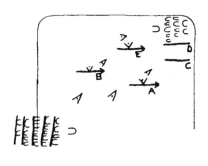

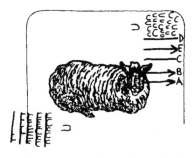

Meanwhile three remaining flats at stage right surreptitiously cross to stage left, approaching the unsuspecting men. As a flat passes downstage of a backwardly traveling dancer, his presence is removed. The flats stack as wings at stage left. One or two men complete their crossing.

I play awake in recognition of my attraction to die.

I conduct a meditation on impermanence to gather the group's energy before the public performance. The rush of adrenalin already on the rise becomes a perfect metaphor for a passing present. It courses through my body. Its heat reddens my face and ears. It swells my flesh and quickens my pulse.

From downstage left a hodgepodge group spring onto the stage. One then another *combination step/leap/jump/flash kick forward* plus *push forward/jerk back, both at once.* Another *combination step/leap/jump flash kick forward* etc., facing upstage right. The entrance is wild but contained. The timing is not slow

or constant. They form a diagonal line from upstage right to downstage left.

"What is it [death], then, if not our destroyer?" I asked.

"Sorcerers say death is the only worthy opponent we have," he replied. *"Death is our challenger. We are born to take that challenge, average men or sorcerers. Sorcerers know about it; average men do not."*

"I personally would say, don Juan, life, not death, is the challenge."

"Life is the process by means of which death challenges us," he said. *"Death is the active force. Life is the arena. And in that arena there are only two contenders at any time: oneself and death."*

—Carlos Castaneda, The Sorcerer

Many more audience members than expected spill down the aisles at the preview. Several people from the Austin School for the Blind and Visually Impaired are given front row seats. I watch the performance from the rear of the house. The extraordinary head and spinal maneuvers necessitated by the visually impaired students to facilitate their seeing gets included in my appreciation of the event onstage.

Together everyone spins 180 degrees, agitates the hands, palms facing, not meeting—palms beating in and out without touching and maybe not rhythm. One leg shoots to the side then crosses way over in front of the other. *Kick out/cross over,* **change legs,** *kick out/cross over,* **change legs, and so on.**

In canon, from down to upstage they *slice open from head to foot down the center of the body.* **The arms fling apart, making an oblique angle to the torso as the body flashes downstage. One leg slides wide open at the same time.** *Slicing open from head to foot down the center of the body* **passes quickly to the person upstage. The movement is highlighted by blowing** *fleesch* **from between the inside of the cheek lining and the outside of the molars, teeth clenched and bared.**

If I perceive this moment as nothing, I am correct. However, if I do not perceive this moment as everything, I am not correct.

I invite being seen as if I were face to face with my beloved. The tangible warmth arising from this intimacy spreads out beyond the confines of my body. The warmth may embrace you as audience. This is not a singular goal but the experience of generosity as movement loosens the boundaries between audience and performer.

The dancers *lock butt* **into place and discharge the body downstage and upstage on the tips of the feet, keeping the buttocks**

fixed. They fall forward, taking tiny rushing steps along the floor. They fall backward, taking tiny rushing steps beyond the balls of the feet. They exit *lock butting*.

By choosing to manifest with less flamboyant or obvious movement, the activity of faith becomes the substance of movement for the dancer.

It is not my living that is not up to par; it is my not remembering to *invite being seen admitting living* that is not up to par.

The stage is empty except for the two choruses, one sitting on benches downstage right and the other standing but not entirely visible upstage left. Conductors signal their choruses to stand. All arms raise, bent, overhead, palms facing, waist-width apart. The entire cast begins traveling, individually, in a clockwise circle; one leg then the other kicks prettily out in front of the body; *1,2,3,4,5, hold, 1,2,3,4,5, hold, 1,2,3,4,5, hold.* The speed and the number of circles made is personal. Sooner or later the dancers arrive upstage and they stand there for a long time.

My dream is greater clarity and more simplicity. I want to walk into a studio and say, "Let us dance," and everyone gathered will understand and proceed without self-consciousness or confusion.

PANS is born again echoing through the dancers; they jump earthward while all other perceptual energy rises in a mushroom-like manner. Gravity or duration hardly count. Arms billow toward the hips; the fingertips soon perch there. With each jump, the sound *PANS* is shaped like petals of a flower in the mouth and similarly released into space. *PANS* is set free—what *snap* will never be. In this manner they arrive midstage.

An "ah ha" is a spontaneously inclusive cosmic shift in perception. DeborAH HAy

With fingertips perched on the hips, they stand quietly together again. Then, *imagining the head where the shins are*, they start tossing it around, keeping the feet on the ground. They avoid translating this movement into a hootchie kootchie or rhumba. While *imagining the head where the shins are* the hands move from the hips to a wing-shape in front of the lips, without the audience noticing. (The audience should be sidetracked by the movement of *imagining the head where the shins are*.) The fingertips of each hand mirror themselves a half-inch apart. With their hand-wings in front of their lips, the performers begin quietly shoveling the word *lamb* back into the mouth as it is expressed. As the movement repeats, it gradually increases in volume before subsiding into silence. This is danced as a group.

A conversation with Brett about the performance artist Linda Montano arises from an event I ask the workshop to attend on the University of Texas campus. Linda is being considered for a full-time faculty position in the art department. She presents two lectures that are open to the public. Brett feels that the context of Linda's performance is entirely self-centered and that therefore she [Brett] does not like it. In comparison Brett believes that what she is learning in the large-group workshop is a more generous arena for the practice of art.

Her response provokes words of caution from me because Linda's public and personal exploration of all levels of consciousness, her readiness to play a rich panorama of entities, is not unlike *inviting being seen whole and changing*. Furthermore, what every human being [whom I know] wants is vital living. Whether it is yoga, travel, basketball, or writing—the goal is vibrancy. I pursue vibrancy in the workshop. I use the studio and the people in it to help me. The plain and simple presence of another human being in the room, his or her unique arrangement of cellular vibration, is supporting my well-being. "If I feel more awake as a result, I will reflect more awake and perhaps you in turn will see and be reminded of playing awake. But that is secondary. I play awake to feel more alive and engaged now. I am that selfish."

With hands poised before the lips, the forty-two artists walk to a predetermined place. Five separate choruses comprise a two-tiered chorale arrangement. Five conductors signal the release of hand-wings from the mouths of their five respective choruses.

What I see enriches me is a simple imaginative game in which what I see stimulates my curiosity and attention to all things.

A chorus of eight, closest to stage right, is conducted by young blond lawyer Becky. Their repertory includes:

1. *De* from "school one day" in the second verse of "Mary Had a Little Lamb." Stop short of the *ay* in "day." The sound is produced as the foot stamps the floor and one hand, held chest high, twists and scoops up from facing down. The twisting wrist action acts as an intermediary for bringing the sound up from the foot and out through the mouth.
2. Two sounds of rain; flatly pat the floor with the feet, and pop the mouth open from loosely held moist lips, opening and closing them like fish.
3. *One* from "school one day, school one day"; blow *one* out of the mouth onto an index finger that is blown forward and returns to be blown by *one* again, or, play the breath from *one* transversely with an index finger interrupting the word's line of fire.

The crying chorus stands beside Becky's. It is led by red-headed, deep-voiced, large-boned, childhood-trained bareback rider Liz Gans. The cries she governs are expressed relatively free of emotional charge. Their repertory includes:

1. One long quiet cry tone is kept alive by the chorus while Liz accentuates with a particularly lusty rendition of *boo hoos.*
2. One hand presses against the belly to focus on the origin of the wail. The other palm circles tightly in the air. The wail is re-

stimulated as the palm recirculates. Loud, long open cries fall down from the world into the receiving singer's thoracic cavity. It waxes and wanes siren-like. When the arm becomes tired, it drops from the elbow in front of the body. It is accompanied by a quickly diminishing wail.

3. Quick jerky breaths rise from the heart out through the nose. Sniffling sobs are accented with short complaining outcries from the throat.

4. The cry that bridges the end of one good sobbing and the beginning of another—it is a low monotonous holding tone squeezed by the throat. It trails off as the lungs press down and release, making bouncy gasps.

5. Fists are tightened in front of the body. A punctuated, irritated expulsion of an endless supply of throat energy pushes the fist forward to punch at the air.

6. The sob of the clown is made with the mouth turned down.

Stage center chorus is made up of five dancers. Its conductor, Manu, is an enigmatic mixture of woman and child. She is the only conductor to face the audience instead of her chorus. They do not sing.

I ask Manu, whose balance on her partial scholarship is in arrears, if she would like to organize the postperformance party at Jerry's in exchange for the remainder of her workshop fee. She is grateful and I am overjoyed. She is experienced at handling food and her Indonesian exoticism touches what we are served.

1. Step to the right and bring the left foot to pause momentarily beside it. Repeat to the left. Continue moving in unison from side to side. It is as close to the air of a black gospel choir as can be rendered by a chorus of two Asians and four Caucasians.

2. The same selection of Turkish names used earlier in the dance

may be intermittently expressed by any of these six chorus members: "Walat," "Vicay," "Beriman," "Hilin," "Recep," "Idris," "Meryem," or "Sinan."

To stage left of the nonsinging chorus are two choruses, one seated in chairs in front of the other standing behind them. Two conductors are present. The sitting conductor commands the sitting chorus; the standing conductor commands the other. Brett conducts the sitting chorus in the following repertory:

1. *Lamb, lamb, lamb, lamb, lamb* is spoken quickly while the hands shovel *lamb* back into the mouth.

The studio altar is dismantled for the last time.

I watch the video of *Lamb, lamb, lamb . . . .* It is a good document. The video crew and costs are entirely paid for through the purchase of cassettes by the people in the workshop.

2. "Tillie's Song" (see page 55):

"Be at the theater no later than 8 a.m. because the front doors will be locked for security reasons."

3. *Mare* from "Mary," stopping short of the *rr* in "Mare."
4. *FLEECSH, FLEECSH* from "fleece was white as snow." Include pressing the ear lobes forward, baring the teeth and sending air forward from the back of the mouth bordered by the outside of the molars and the inside flesh of the cheeks.

Impermanence is seeing infinity altering inconsequentially.

Standing behind the seated chorus at a choral angle (left shoulder turned slightly toward its conductor Sheelah Murthy) are the last twelve dancers. They are conducted in the following songs:

1. A short *o* from "white as snow"—an o for every snowflake song.
2. Attach the *LL* from "follow" to the *OO* from "school." *LL* is

expressed with the chin pressing forward and up. *OO* drops down to the bottom of the inside of the mouth as the head slides down to the right shoulder. It peaks back to center with the chin and the *LL* then slides back down to *OO* on the left side. *LL-OO* is sung as a unit.

3. Throw *he he he he he* from the chest into an elliptical orbit that returns to the mouth.

When I recognize my same old dancing self wearing the pants, I shift into 50 trillion cells changing and my outfit vanishes.

4. Shoot the breath across the top of an extended lower lip; high-speed particles shoot up through the feet and out across the lip. The tongue acts like a spring inside the mouth.

Linda Montano gives another talk at the university this afternoon, and I see many people from the workshop, even some who aren't in class this morning. They greet me without a trace of guilt or embarrassment. Being in class everyday is the guiding principle for the workshop. It is grounds for dismissal. I experience shock and then betrayal. Fortunately Sister Rosita (Linda Montano) is administering holy water during her lecture. I stand in line with other sinners in the audience who are seeking absolution, and I am cleansed of my hostility. Perhaps my students were cleansed of their guilt before I arrived.

5. Sing *la la la la la la la la la lalalalala* liltingly;
6. With open mouth and hollow chest, slap the flat of the hand onto the sternum. Listen to it.

Most of us remain in the theater to sit in silent meditation following the public performance. Our silence is tangibly satisfying. The meditation is the deepest I ever experience. My consciousness smoothly shifts from skeletal to universal, nothing to everything to nothing again. I am reduced, expanded, and held in both, all at once.

Why is group stillness not a postperformance tradition? What better way is there to benefit from the rush of human chemistry than to savor it in silence after its bouquet is released?

I remember the Sunset Tour of Ayers Rock in central Australia. Ayers Rock is a sacred site for the aboriginal people. It is also a desert landscape tourist attraction. I find thousands of chattering tourists facing west with cameras. How many years will it be in the evolution of humankind before we understand the dynamics of the choice to be silent together?

The five choruses converge, plaintively calling *Mare*, without reaching the *rr* sound. Conductors become chorus as they now turn to face the audience.

This is the choreographer's cue to walk to the stage from the audience. Dressed in white, she steps into the role of conductor. She slowly raises her arms and begins to lead the full chorus in a melodious rendition of "Mary Had a Little Lamb":

Mary had a little lamb, little lamb, little lamb
Mary had a little lamb, its fleece was white as snow.
Everywhere that Mary went, Mary went, Mary went
Everywhere that Mary went, the lamb was sure to go.

The choreographer, dressed in white, steps into the role of conductor. She slowly raises her arms and begins to lead the full chorus in a melodious rendition of "Mary Had a Little Lamb."

As I conduct the chorus at the conclusion of each performance, I think I can hear the dance suddenly clicking into place in the minds of the audience behind me.

What comes into the choreographer from this relationship to chorus and audience thrills her no end. She is finally, for the first time in her life, in a role that everyone understands, and she feels blinded by power.

Later, we dive into the pale blue waters of a stone-sculpted pool with a waterfall crowning one end. Small groups of dancers relax in and depart from the hot tub beside the pool. Steam rises. The moon is full. Planets burn. A lamb piñata hangs from a thick tree limb above the patio. Taking turns, we blindly target the papier-maché lamb with a long pole, and sometimes sticky candies fly to the ground. Scott Heron coaxes me to the patio to take my turn. I feel like an idiot with an axe. After several thwacks, I step back to remove the blindfold and am handed the papier-maché lamb's head. I am the executioner.

Split drop,
point pop,
Ah ha
nada.

Afterword

Poignant undefinable references arise from the choreography as I watch the public performances of *Lamb, lamb, lamb, lamb . . . .* I want to taste every detail of the movement. I want to perform everyone's part, separately and in all combinations. This deeper penetration into the physical, theatrical, and metaphysical body of the dance is where my solo begins. During *Playing Awake 1992* I choreograph a solo for seventeen dancers.

I do not know exactly when the performance meditation *living and dying at once* metamorphoses into *ah ha/nada, perceived insepa- rably*. When *Playing Awake 1992* begins, the physical integration of the new metaphor has so impressed itself on me that it is easily assimilated by the workshop—although there are days when all meaning is lost.

Ah ha/nada reduces language to sound and music. Thinking is not translatable. When I try to conceptualize "ah ha," "nada" makes the effort meaningless.

I look around the studio. The music is blaring, people are engaged everywhere, yet there is no indication that a dance workshop is in progress. At these times the core of my being becomes so unteth- ered that laughter is the only recourse for my sanity. Like the day Grace Mi-He Lee and I are turned upside down in the same door- way, one leg each, waving in the air, our arms press into the door jamb and each other's body for support. The longer we practice *ah ha/nada* from this vantage point, the more hysterical we become.

From the outside it is impossible to determine that discipline is being advanced. Theoretically, I consider this a step in the evolu- tion of dance. Personally, it feels like my limits are exploding.

People are in groups. They are talking, screaming, acting within scenarios, teasing, playing anything and everything. A few students sleep covered with blankets used in the yoga class that precedes the workshop.

A few dancers have difficulty with those who sleep. Discipline, in their minds, requires attention, acuity, vitality; it looks like something. I choose, with the experience of twelve annual large-group workshops behind me, to democratize the tangible and intangible dynamics of discipline. There is no way discipline looks. As a matter of fact, I am as challenged by the person sleeping as the dancer dancing. The dancer lying down with a blanket over her or his body dares to tempt judgment. I am inspired and moved by this demonstration of faith in the workshop process.

Either create an environment where everyone looks alike, where surface is untested, where technique is obvious, translatable, and clear; or, in the context of dance, create room for disorder, where movements cannot be learned and everyone is a special mystery. Here the observer can stretch and be served by all odds.

A letter from Heleri following *Playing Awake 1992:*

> I look at the video of the preview. I have imagined myself far different than what I see. I imagined myself dancing with confidence, not so different, so much older looking than all the rest. I seem always to have a question mark, what comes next? My steps are short and tight, tight all over except my arms which are flabby. My head rests on my shoulders without neck in between. The mirror did not make obvious what the video does. I should be dancing only for myself, not in public. Perhaps I do dance well sometimes. It is when I feel part of the creative process, not always even then. I am left frustrated, out of place. Last year I could hide. In *Lamb at the Altar,* I have no place to go. Because I imagined myself 'adequate,' I am now ashamed. I face a reality I have avoided. Perhaps that is all I have learned. I am old, slowed down, stiff, forgetful, dependent on others, hard of hearing, dim of vision physical and mental, somehow defeated. And that defeat is a kind of success. It binds me to the rest of humanity. It just took me a little bit longer to see it.
>
> Heleri

I immediately respond to Heleri's letter and tell her that if I stopped dancing when I first saw myself on video, my career would have ended just when in fact it truly began.

This isn't to say that what Heleri sees is not true. I watch Thursday evening's preview performance as it is videotaped and muse, "Maybe Heleri's performance days *are* numbered." Throughout the workshop she fears her inability to remember the sequence of movements. She invents stories to help her connect phrases; she makes index cards with drawings for Beverly to flash from a distance. Other dancers become guides if she appears lost. Anyone can talk to her during the dance. Nothing placates her fear of memory loss. The closer the performances, the more panic she exhibits. She looks lost and tired the evening the video is shot with a live audience present. Once this first performance is over, without any mishap on her part, she resumes her confidence and flair and performs the following three nights with the grace and humor only an eighty-one-year-old woman can embody.

"But even if you had had an absolutely exquisite performance that night, Heleri, I propose this to you: the sensitivity required to capture a performer choosing to live her dying in front of a camera is impossibly ephemeral to achieve. Don't stop performing. The humor, sobriety, and physicality of your spirit is a measure of living that deserves to be regarded."

Very few people from the Austin community attend the April weekend performances of *Lamb at the Altar*. Perhaps it is because of Good Friday, Passover, and Easter Sunday. I think some who choose to be or not be audience do not realize how much their presence adds to a performance. For an experimental movement artist there are few avenues of gratification other than the presence of an audience.

On Easter Sunday there are never more than a dozen audience members beside the performers and their families.

In the lobby approaching the entrance to the studio are four altars, created by individuals from the workshop. They are as different from one another as pink is from black, mirror from stone, ragdoll from virgin, bouquet from diorama. Through the doorway, along the hallway leading to an entry room with an exit to the back porch, is another altar made with childrens' drawings, rocks, and stones. Moments before this altar is completed, Phil Conard, electrician and friend, flies into the studio, uncalled for and nearly unnoticed, and proceeds to install a four-foot-long blue neon tube in the ceiling above the rock altar. Meanwhile, Herb and Heleri, who collaborate on this altar, are picking around the supply room for clamp-on lights or candles.

Beverly and I sweep, clean, and rearrange the long narrow loading dock that runs almost the width of the building. In an hour it metamorphoses from an abandoned responsibility to a tidy and leisurely environment for Easter Sunday appreciation. Facing the railroad tracks are fifteen supermarket lawn chairs borrowed from Beverly's wedding seating decor from five years ago. Yawning open, they sit soaped, rinsed, and already dry in the steamy post-rainstorm afternoon. Hawkeye's mother contributes a stunning spread of breads, fruits, cheeses, and cookies. (Hawkeye fell out of a tree and broke his back six months before the workshop began. Until he fell, he moved like an eagle. His participation in the workshop with his recent limitations takes on special meaning for everyone.) A large crock of iced tea miraculously lasts into the night. I know because I drink the last cup. Three or four small garden tables with chairs tucked around them hug the edge of the porch. Wildflowers are placed everywhere.

The attraction to the backporch is to sit back, relax, and watch one of the twenty or more trains that go by between 2 p.m. and 11:30 p.m. The audience is encouraged to leave and return to the performance at will. A ticket today means a twelve-hour pass to the event. No one is expected to remain for the entire twelve hours. Each member of the workshop is to perform the thirty-five minute solo *Lamb at the Altar*. A week ago, names were drawn from a brown paper bag to determine the order. I perform at six o'clock.

Beverly and I, with enough fabric between us to cover every chair comprising the seating area, devise a color scheme, divide the cloths into one of three color themes, and proceed to drape five rows of tiered folding chairs—golds down the middle, reds to one side, and blues on the other. Under the gelled lights the area becomes a lavish tapestry altar for the audience.

Across the back wall of the stage are twenty-five white sheets that hang with their bottom edges just touching the floor; each upper edge is stapled to one-by-two-inch wooden slats, which are suspended by fishing line from the ceiling. Both sides of the stage are also occupied by a floating arrangement of pressed white sheets. There are forty sheets in all. Scott Lehman from last year's workshop designs the studio, continuing last year's theme of floating flats.

The performance begins at 2 p.m., and Herb is preparing himself thoughtfully and quietly. A few of the audience are present. Composer Ellen Fullman is in full force, having had the three prior performances to work out any kinks in her electronic engineering wizardry.

We, the performers, run the lights for each other for two reasons. Firstly, there are no funds for a lighting designer, and secondly, the large number of blackouts and fade-outs makes it seem easier to keep this job in the family. Many of us use a lightboard for the first time.

For every solo there is one performer dancing, one running the lights, and another who executes the crashes. Three crashes, used to confuse the audience and to propel the dancer back onstage the moment of exit, occur at various places in the dance. Ellen supplies three flimsy tripods with hooks, two pails, a trash can cover, and two long plastic tubes. One tube is the club used to dismantle or smash the restacked materials. By evening's end, chips of black and silver paint cover the crash site, and the tripods and pails lie inert and mutilated.

We are dressed in garments that Daniélè Massie, wardrobe consultant, has selected from our closets. With some, her choice is immediate and irrevocable. With others she picks over the "costumes" until the last minute and even after one, two, or three of the performances.

I don't believe that any of us imagine having a great tolerance for watching *Lamb at the Altar* for twelve hours straight. We have been looking at it daily for the last four months. But when Herb takes it upon himself to begin exactly at 2 p.m., we are all present, seated, and quiet. I believe he catches us off-guard with his punctilious start. He is personable and clear. I feel like I am watching an engineer or a car mechanic. Saraja follows, and here is where I feel the stage is set for what becomes a timeless rite of passage for everyone in the workshop. Saraja's performance is vastly different but as impeccable as Herb's in the ways she figures prominently within each moment in the story of her dance. And thus it happens that each of us meets this final performance of *Lamb at the Altar* with thoughtful and poetic skill. As the constituency of this practice, we follow each dance with admiration and glee.

Ellen, meanwhile, is stationed at her table stacked with electronics and keyboard. Fortunately there are long periods of silence integral to the dance, so she has some opportunities to rest. At 10:30 p.m., seated high on the last row, I feel someone tap me from behind. As I lean down, Ellen whispers with an air of disbelief that often colors our conversations, "Deborah, you always ask me to do the craziest things!" We are so tired and so happy to be so keyed into so many lives at once that we spill over laughing, noiselessly, shaking loose some of the enormous tension from this stunning performance vigil.

Lamb at the Altar

dedicated to John Cage

choreographed and performed by Deborah Hay

music: Ellen Fullman

premiere: October 1, 1992

Warren Street Performance Loft,

New York City

Key to Illustrations

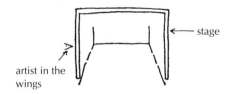

stage

artist in the wings

grid = stop here
  travel here
  direction traveled

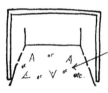

indicates the direction the performer is facing

circle indicates where a movement is performed in place and direction the dancer is facing

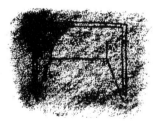

BLACKOUT

A sense of intimacy is cast by house and stage lights as the audience enters the theater.

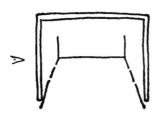

She stands in the wings waiting for the lights onstage to brighten. This is her cue to begin the dance.

Bent forward, taking fine, quick little steps, she incorporates *sneaking* to shape her passage across stage.

She stops, aware of the angle she is perceived by the audience while she is seeing what lies within her view of the stage.

The recorded music begins.

Her movements are influenced by the performance of an eighty-year-old woman practiced at *baton twirling*.

[Heleri was a short, round, sweet-faced eighty-year-old trapeze artist, marathon walker, and mountain climber with beautiful legs.]

She is the *baton twirling*, its tips, an atom of baton tossed in the air.

She switches direction, aware of being perceived in profile while she sees what lies within *this* view of the stage.

Her dance includes Brenda; plump, Puerto Rican, and proud.

[Three weeks before the performances of *Lamb, lamb, lamb . . .* , Brenda became ill with a rare inner ear virus that kept her bed-ridden. Brenda's plump expansive body hampered by dizziness, queazy stomach, and long convalescence presented a naturally less articulate baton-twirler.]

She is influenced by the memory of Brenda's baton twirling, vertigo, and disinterest. She exits performing *some-of-Brenda*, her baton, and her twirling. She dwells near the wing before vanishing.

BLACKOUT

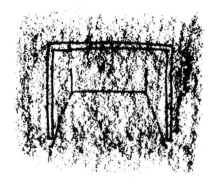

She quickly returns to stage and assumes a crouched posture, her torso bent forward at the waist.

LIGHTS UP

Her movement includes the *warm-pressure-of-a-free-spirited-twirler's-hand-clutching-a-baton.*

She pivots continuing the *gentle-pressure-of-a-hand-clutching-a-baton* dance. Exiting, facing one direction but traveling another, she *dwells* near the wing before exiting.

The moment she disappears a LOUD CRASH is heard from off-stage.

LOUD CRASH

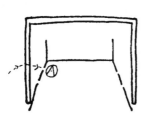

She reappears performing one *tail-end-of-a-jump.*

Elevated on half-toe, she lifts her knee to initiate each step as she proceeds down to the tip of the stage. With each step she tries to define a new world that includes seeing, form, and realignment. Her elevation and her proximity to the wall (or wings) interfere with her ability to be definitive.

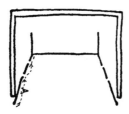

Pivoting, her arms stretch overhead. She yanks her thigh to her chest then immediately releases it. Her foot seeks a flat and rapid return to the stage floor. She *drifts* from the wall (or wings) to which she just clung, making an *obscure return* upstage.

Again, elevated on half-toe, lifting her knee to begin each step, she presses along an invisible diagonal wall from upstage to down. With each step she attempts to define a new reality, but her elevation and proximity to the invisible wall interfere with her intentions.

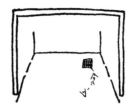

Weight returns to her feet. Her arms open and curve out to her sides while her head *remains without stillness.* Her legs, *without definition,* *blossom* from her body. *Everywhere-at-once*, she purposely *drifts* upstage one step at a time.

She stops. Her head faces right then left, continuously, as her spine slips vertically toward the floor. She is singing *Tillie's song*.

[Tillie, age 71, shared my daughter Savannah's hospital room in February '91. This was Tillie's first hospital stay. The staff said she was mentally retarded. Until her mentally retarded sister died two years ago, she lived with her. Now she lived alone. She was impatient to get home after a mild colon surgery. Tillie continually spoke sense and nonsense words to herself. Sitting with Savannah on the bed next to Tillie's, I could not help listening, charmed by her jabber. The tone expressed enthusiasm for what was spoken and a real other person who listened and responded. Her talk was imbued with love. Chuckles, considerations, asides, wove through her language. Real words jumped out now and then.]

The movement concludes frantically, to distract the sight of her buttocks contacting the floor.

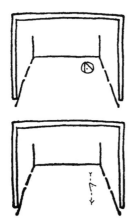

Her legs stretch forward. She presses her hands into the floor on either side of her hips and lifts herself just enough to *scootch* her body downstage. Everything suggests she is traveling backward diagonally but she is advancing directly downstage.

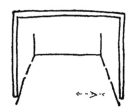

Pivoting right, she pulls her flattened legs around with her. She resumes *scootching* backward before *spiraling up* from the floor.

Fake triplets snap her from the spiral. Her path becomes inverted and curvaceous. One hand touches the elbow of the opposite arm. Her arms switch back and forth like this at whim.

The *fake triplets* end with both hands, one on top of the other, poised under her chin. Quietly, she stands facing the audience for the first time.

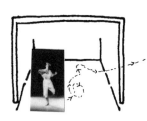

Her body is the altar that supports her soul. She plays *lamb at the altar.*

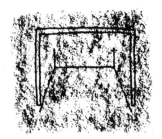

From nowhere comes a *trace-of-a-waltz*; a moment in a child's dream; a *fraction-of-spin*, a *millisecond-of-swirl*, a *glimpse-of-gliding*. She exits *not-entirely-waltz-ing.*

LIGHTS OUT

LIGHTS ON

She is seen *sneaking* across stage. She pivots 180 degrees. Hunched forward at the waist, she propels herself through space pushing backward with her hips while she kicks forward and down with her legs. If the stage surface permits, she plants rhythms on the floor with the help of the kidskin soles of her acrobatic sandals. Just before she exits she breaks into *fake choreography.*

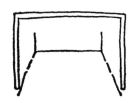

EXIT

LOUD CRASH OFFSTAGE

She jumps back onto the stage performing *"PANS."*

[Savannah Bradshaw and Heather Jarry, two twenty-year-old, long-limbed and kinky-haired beauties, entered jumping earthward onto their girls' legs as the remainder of their attention mushroomed upward. As they jumped, their hands billowed toward their hips, eventually perching there. With each jump the sound "PANS" was shaped like petals of a flower and similarly set free in space from their unsprung female voices. Similarly fragile in countenance, they hardly appeared to exist in gravity or duration. "PANS" was a breath spoken—not a word. It is the opposite of 'snap'.]

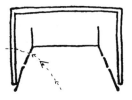

The last *"PANS"* leaves her downstage center. Aware of making-it-look-like-she-is-seduced-by-her-body, she isn't. She is getting ready to conduct the audience to join her in singing *Mary Had a Little Lamb*. They join her.

She chooses an arbitrary moment to exit while the audience is still singing. They are the accompaniment for her weight-less exit.

EXIT

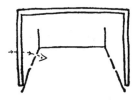

She instantly reappears close-to-the-stage-floor performing *not-somersault-ing*. She is a fraction of a memory pro-longed performing *not-somersaulting*.

She *rises* from the floor. Each hand is cupped, fingertips converged and poised at each temple. Elbows stick out from her head. With weight on one straight leg, the other is bent at the knee with the length of its toes resting on the floor. Her torso curves right and left as she sashays from right to left, pausing between change of direction. Her movement contains the memory of Panamanian Marta, a vision of simplicity and virtue.

[Her movement registered in an effortless and most direct way. Marta manifested as a gentle and virtuous being—dark eyes, very short black curly hair, a small nose, and rosebud lips. Her body was thin, lanky, undisturbed. As a friend said of *Lamb, lamb, lamb, lamb...,* "When I thought I didn't know what was going on I looked at Marta and understood. This happened without thinking."]

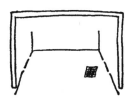

In the middle of a sashay she slips into *runfloating*—moments retained from childhood. She does not cover distance. Expanse is where she is.

She turns out of *runfloating*—short, soft jump turns, knees relaxed. Her body turns in one direction while her arms travel in the opposite direction.

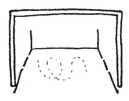

She recalls her torso to vertical, crying "ha," jumping proudly, showing her palms, and remaining poised throughout. Her energy does not alter at the end of a jump or "ha." Following the third "ha" the lights begin to fade. By the sixth "ha" the stage and house are dark.

FADE TO BLACK

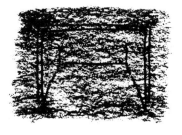

LIGHTS UP

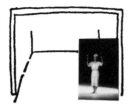

She faces the audience with maracas overhead in each hand, anticipating the right moment to release them into song.

She plays them.

Her playing ends abruptly. *Gaily-doing-nothing-much*, while in fact performing *lamb at the altar*, her cavort takes her from stage into the audience. In this manner the audience is provided with an intermission.

She returns to stage and resumes the Panamanian Marta posture again; fingertips at each temple, elbows spread from her head, torso curved right or left with one leg straight and the other bent, heel off the floor.

She calls "Mare" but stops short of forming the rr sound. Mare is the first sound in *Mary Had a Little Lamb*. She shapes the sound with love. She calls several times, pausing in between each "Mare." She maintains Marta's influence on her.

In the middle of the last "Mare" she says "dd." "Dd" is the end of the second word from *Mary Had a Little Lamb*. Each time she sings "dd" her cupped fingertips drop down from her temples to stop on an intermittent path toward her sides.

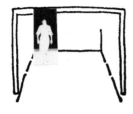

Finally she drops her arms, releasing her palms open, arching her head back and pressing one leg out further than the other in front of her body. She performs this quickly, before swiveling into the next movement.

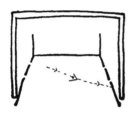

Facing left, she *etches-her-profile* in space. One leg lunges forward while the other remains bent or extended behind. Her arms, bent at the elbows, alternate one-in-front-one-behind her torso which either leans forward or is upright. Her hands and fingers arch, circle, and curl under her chin and at her spine. Occasionally she will drop her weight into both knees then spring back to a lunge position.

When the *tip of her nose touches the edge of the stage,* she automates into robot-like movement. She does not become mechanical although she plays as close as possible to looking so.

Midway to stage center she slows down to a halt, as if a battery died; a few winding-up noises and she proceeds to center stage.

Facing the audience she throws her head all the way back, drops her arms straight to her side, thrusts one leg out in front of her body, and stays a very long time. This is the most clear example of *lamb at the altar* for the artist and the audience.

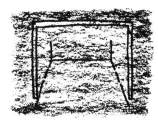

In one great swoop her head and torso swing upright and lead her into a 180 degree turn repeating the *mock-robot* movement. Facing upstage she again throws her head back but stays only briefly—just long enough for the audience to think she will repeat the long pose—but she doesn't. Instead her arms rise grandly from her sides to overhead. She draws them together reverentially and stops. Slowly turning to the audience with *nothing more to do*, she drops her arms to her sides. The stage and house fade to darkness as she looks at the audience.

FADE OUT

LIGHTS UP

She is already in motion along a large clockwise path. Leaping with her legs in front of her, she throws her head back while fanning her arms overhead before slapping her hands onto her thighs or stopping them midflight. Although there is no rhythm or order surrounding this ritualistic-looking dance, it seems like there is.

She completes the circle with both arms still in the air and, facing the audience, begins *laughing and crying at once.* She laughs/cries in three locations, suspending the volume of her cry as she transits, quickly tiptoeing to each new place. She appreciates the opportunity to fit laughing and crying into one moment.

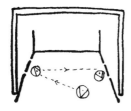

In the middle of the third cry she cuts into a lightweight prancing movement that hardly travels forward at all. Her hands are poised, palms facing, overhead and waist-width apart from one another. It takes a long time for her to traverse space. She does not decide where to travel. She listens for direction and the opportunity to exit.

EXIT

LOUD CRASH IN THE WINGS

She reappears, *lopsided*—as if something disturbed the strong verticality observed in the former movement. Askew, legs three feet apart, she crosses stage, not knowing but curious about how to travel with these limitations.

The moment she arrives she *is finished.* She drops her arms and looks at the audience.

FADE TO DARKNESS

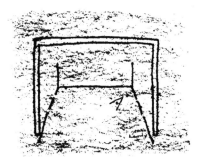

The direction she faces is shifted.

LIGHTS UP

Although barely moving physically except to adjust her posture—to indicate that she in fact is turning (on some other level), she turns, her arms at her sides.

Attempting to dislodge her own altar, and

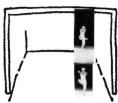

others in the theater, she shouts "POP," throwing her arms and body forward. Several "POP"s are performed to try and catch herself and the audience unaware.

On the last "POP" she throws her arms forward but does not cry aloud. The fingertips return, touching her neck and stopping. They press forward again, one hand returning to her breast and one to a rib. The next time her hands slip inside her knees, spreading them apart carefully. Her fingertips then release and point down just above the tops of her feet. She is *curled and balled* forward and down.

From below the surface of the floor, energy travels up through her feet and out through her mouth at which point she delicately places an "o" in space. It is the "o" from "its fleece was white as snow." She curls forward again to the floor, then brings up another "o" when it is ready.

The last time she uncurls, her arms are carried overhead and instead of a child's "o," she mourns "o." She *weeps her arms down* to her hips, grateful for an altar that can rock with the sound of sorrow.

The moment her fingertips touch her hip bones she begins to prance, her lower

legs flipping up behind her. She prances five times, just out of rhythm, and then pauses. *Five prances and a pause*, again and again.

Halfway through the last set of five prances she jumps, leaving the floor just enough to jump, and stops. At the same time she snaps her fingers, says "snap," then releases her fists. Movement and sound are performed as fast as humanly possible. Her challenge is to perform "*snap*" before anyone, including herself, realizes its tiny lifetime.

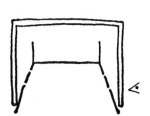

She "*snaps*" several times traveling backward before her weight collapses into her knees, her body breaking in a descending jagged pattern as she rapidly exits remaining on her feet.

She *stays* in the wings longer than expected.

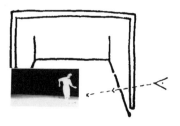

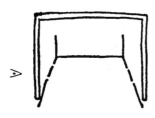

Taking tiny elevated steps while turning counterclockwise she crosses stage before collapsing again into a descending path that now carries her off-stage right.

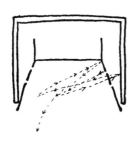

She *stays* in the wings longer than expected.

Nearly out-of-control, she reappears turning, before springing into "*PANS.*"

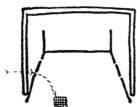

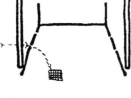

She *ducks* and ducking *snakes* her way upstage left to the edge of the wing.

Pulling her hands to her lips she blows them forward breathing out the word "one." Her leg rises, the toes brushing upward along her standing leg before opening and carrying her forward, half running to keep up with the breath of "one." She retreats back into or to the edge of the wing before blowing "one" again. Quiet candor is exhibited in the performance and repetition of the "one" movement. The final "one" takes her into the audience.

She steps onto half-toe with legs apart. Her arms stretch out from her shoulders. Holding onto this tenuous position she calls "little." Her mouth and lips are spread so wide that it sounds like "leetle." Her mouth drops to its normal position after each "leetle" is pronounced. "Lee-tle" is expressed with love.

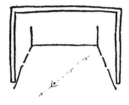

She craftily guides the attention of the audience back onto stage with her. Stepping backward on one leg, the other is drawn to it as if measuring space with the movement. Her arms, lifted, help guide her path to the far upstage left corner of the stage. *Looking like she is facing one direction, she faces many.*

She swivels to face the audience stepping forward into a wide lunging stance. Both arms stretch diagonally forward from her body. Her hands return to her mouth, scooping the word "lamb" back into it as it falls out. Her entire mouth, jaw, and tongue are used to express "lamb." She steps forward again, performing *"lamb"* intermittently until the lights fade to darkness.

SLOW FADE TO DARKNESS

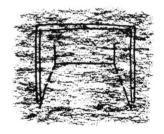

Born in Brooklyn in 1941, Deborah Hay began her
career with the Judson Dance Theater and the
Merce Cunningham Dance Company in the 1960s.
In the early 1970s, she created a series of Ten Circle
Dances, which were collected in the book *Moving
through the Universe in Bare Feet.* Since 1976 she
has lived in Austin, Texas, where she conducts
annual large-group workshops, each lasting four
months and culminating in public performances.
Hay received a Guggenheim Fellowship for Choreography in 1983 and has been awarded numerous
National Endowment for the Arts Choreographer
Fellowships. She has performed and taught workshops in Europe, Canada, Mexico, Australia, and
throughout the United States. Her writings appear in
The Drama Review and *Contact Quarterly.*

Library of Congress Cataloging-in-Publication Data
Deborah Hay
Lamb at the altar: the story of a dance / Deborah Hay
ISBN 0-8223-1448-7. —ISBN 0-8223-1439-8 (pbk.)
1. Lamb, lamb (Dance)   1993   792.8'42—dc20
93-21063 CIP